A

BETTER

WAY

TO

RETIRE

A BETTER WAY TO RETIRE

How a Fiduciary Retirement Planner Can Be the Key to Financial Success

Copyright © 2025 Frankie Guida

ISBN (paperback): 978-1-964046-86-0
ISBN (hardcover): 978-1-964046-93-8

Editing by Caroline Banton
Copyediting by Lucy Spencer
Proofreading by Geena Barret
Cover design and book design by Paperback Expert

A BETTER WAY TO RETIRE

How a Fiduciary Retirement Planner
Can Be the Key to Financial Success

FRANKIE GUIDA, CFP®

Disclaimer:

Advisory services are offered through A Better Way Financial, LLC, an investment advisor in the state of Pennsylvania. Insurance products and services are offered through ABWI, LLC, an affiliated company.

All content is for information purposes only. It is not intended to provide any tax or legal advice or provide the basis for any financial decisions, nor is it intended to be a projection of current or future performance or indication or future results. Purchases are subject to suitability. This requires a review of an investor's objective, risk tolerance, and time horizons. Investing always involves risk and possible loss of capital. This book illustrates examples of client stories. This is for informational purposes only and results may vary based on an individual's circumstance.

*I dedicate this book to my clients.
My profession exists only because of
you. Without the continued trust and
confidence you have placed in me, I
would not possess the knowledge I have.
What's more, I would not have been able
to put this book and our experiences into
words. Thank you!*

*I appreciate and cherish the relationships
and friendships I have gained. Lastly,
I look forward to our continued
partnership and success.*

CONTENTS

ACKNOWLEDGMENTS

Thanks to my parents, Frank and Kimberly, for the opportunity to enter the field of retirement planning. I am proud to serve the community in the way they have for so many years.

To Jade. You are an amazing woman and partner. I am blessed God has made you part of my life, and I am excited and honored to experience my journey through life with you.

INTRODUCTION

I want people to feel that they are valued. . . . I'm cooking food from my home, from meals I've had in my family. I tell them the stories of the dishes. I'm taking their hand and taking them along. My aim is for you to leave feeling like someone had embraced you. That's how food should be.
—Asma Khan

I have read countless books that claim to provide the answers to the challenges people face in life. However, before I invest the time, I like to make sure that the book applies to me. In that spirit, and to respect your time, I want to start by making it clear who I see as the audience for this book.

If you are in your fifties or older and actively planning for retirement, then this book is for you. It can show how to set yourself up for financial stability and a rewarding retirement by having a plan aiming to create multiple streams of income. This book is designed to guide you along the path that you are on or help you choose a better alternative. I will lay out the steps you can take to improve your retirement planning efforts.

Do you like to be proactive and take control of your own financial planning? Do you use Excel sheets or budgeting software? If so, kudos to you. You are an example to us all! However, I will tell you that this book is also for you.

Taking a proactive approach to finances is wise, but taking a totally independent approach is not. You can plan for retirement by yourself, but I have a few good reasons why you shouldn't.

First, many of my clients are able and conscientious and have initially done their own financial planning. Some show me impressive spreadsheets they have developed. They consider potential economic downturns, inflation, Roth conversions, and even the effect of income on their IRMAA brackets. They even consider their life expectancy based on their DNA. These clients share their personal visions for retirement. But even with such forethought, they overlook significant factors.

Second, the clients I see who fall into this category sooner or later realize there is something missing in their financial planning. That something is an asset they cannot possess. As retail investors, although they may be knowledgeable, they lack access to the "tools of the trade." By that I mean institutional-level investment products and AI-driven predictive financial planning software. One of the biggest advantages of working with a financial planner is the powerful resources and tools we have at hand. We can access investment products, data, and analytics the common investor cannot get, or at least that would not be feasible for them to purchase.

Third, financial planning takes time, and it might not be cost-effective for you to use your time trying to navigate unknown territory. Why not employ someone who knows that territory inside and out? Why not work with someone who can guide you confidently through it?

Fourth, what happens if you or your spouse take control of the financial planning but then one of you passes away? One spouse is then left to fend for themselves. It's better to have an additional partner that you can both rely on. Also, as you age, you become less sharp. Decisions may seem more difficult to make. They may even be overwhelming in a rapidly changing world.

I am a fiduciary retirement planner. This title is distinct from a non-fiduciary retirement planner, financial advisor, or broker. As a fiduciary, I work with my clients' interests in mind at all times. I embark with my clients on a path to retirement while clearly explaining any potential conflicts of interest. I am more than a financial advisor because I focus on retirement planning, not wealth-building. I am not a broker because I am not selling specific investment products. A broker can be a good fit for those looking to do their own investments since they typically charge a commission only on transactions, but for those looking for more comprehensive retirement planning, they may not be the best fit.

In this book, I will explain what I do and why. I will explore the strategies I frequently suggest and open up to my clients. I divulge DIY (do-it-yourself) investing knowledge that gives my clients advantages—advantages they would not otherwise have as an independent retail investor.

Retirement brings on many first-time events, such as turning on Social Security, selecting a Medicare plan, and planning for required minimum distributions. Retirement can also mean taking the right pension option at the right time—that is, if you are still fortunate enough to have a pension. As you approach retirement, a well-thought-out plan will help reduce your exposure to high-risk investments such as equities. It can include suitable estate and tax planning strategies.

This book addresses each and all of the important aspects of retirement planning. So that nothing falls through the cracks, it offers a road map. The map shows how to set yourself up for an excellent financial quality of life in your retirement years. It can help to relieve the stress so many people feel about their financial situation and retirement planning.

My family has Italian roots, and traditions are important to us. Sunday dinners as a family are one of these traditions. We love to gather as a family, converse, cook, and enjoy recipes passed down through generations.

Traditions and recipes have been handed down for generations in the Guida family, but not all of them involve food. Helping people retire is another Guida family tradition with its own "recipe." The original recipe was created by my father, as he worked to help families prepare for their retirement. This original recipe has been refined over several decades of learning and improvement, all leading to the practice we have today.

As the next generation, I am honored by the privilege of preserving our family recipe and continuing to serve clients the "dish" of optimism and peace of mind about their future.

We see many similarities between the warm tradition of sharing family meals and the tradition of sharing meaningful conversations with our clients. So in the pages that follow, you'll notice food-themed quotations at the start of each chapter. These epigraphs reveal unexpected connections between cooking a mouth-watering dish and planning a much-anticipated retirement. I hope you enjoy learning about our family recipe for *A Better Way to Retire.*

1

DON'T DO IT ALONE WHEN PLANNING FOR RETIREMENT

To eat is a necessity, but to eat intelligently is an art.
—François de la Rochefoucauld

I entered the retirement planning business because my parents were fiduciaries. I grew up watching them serve their clients and their families. I have learned that fiduciary retirement planning is not just about money, it's about helping families deal with life's challenges. Those challenges could be helping and protecting their family, paying for college, combating inflation, or protecting themselves from paying extra in taxes. They could be caring for aging parents or navigating health issues. They could be figuring out when to turn on Social Security or which option to select on a pension.

When I was sixteen, my mother saw me working on my resume, and she asked me what type of job I was looking for. I told her I didn't know. She said there was plenty of work at my dad's office.

I began working at the family firm as an intern. I fetched coffee, baked cookies, filed papers, and learned some of the back-office tasks. There was QuickBooks, scheduling, and IT troubleshooting.

One day, I noticed that people who left after a conference meeting with my dad appeared less anxious than when they came in. They emerged from his office relaxed—smiling in most cases—as though a weight had been lifted from their shoulders.

I wondered what my dad was doing to have this effect on people. I asked him if I could sit in on some of his meetings to try to learn more. He thought it would be great for me to sit in and take notes.

One day, a lady met with my dad. She arrived in a state that I can only describe as very anxious. During her meeting with my dad, she told him she was afraid that she would run out of money. She was a recent widow, and her husband had taken care of the finances. She explained that she was too scared to spend money. She was invited to take day trips with her friends or eat out, but she always felt she had to refuse for fear of overspending. I felt sorry for her and wondered if she was going to be okay.

As this was going on, my dad sat there calm, cool, and collected. Fortunately, he had already run the numbers using financial planning software to see whether she was on track with her retirement. He was able to deliver some outstanding news. By my dad's calculations, she could live comfortably in her retirement on the income she currently had. Moreover, with the planning we did for her, she would have $20,000 more in income each year projected for the rest of her life. The woman cried tears of joy hearing that she could return to living her life and doing what she really wanted to do. From that moment on, I no longer saw this work as a job. I saw it as an opportunity to be a career where I could help people make their lives better.

I graduated from Bucknell University with a degree in economics and a minor in Italian. I spent the latter part of my senior year and my first year out of college studying day and night for the CFP® exam. I passed the exam on my first attempt and became one of the youngest CFP® professionals in the country.[1] The average age of

---

1   "CFP® Professional Demographics," CFP Board, last updated November 1, 2025, https://www.cfp.net/industry-insights/reports-and-statistics/professional-demographics.

certification for CFP® professionals at the time was 49. I was 24.

Since then, I have put all my energy into learning about investments, income, and tax planning options so that I can better serve my clients. I try to make these complicated topics simpler for those not in the finance field.

There are questions that practically all people have regarding planning for retirement. These are some of the most common questions:

Am I saving enough for retirement?
The answer to this question depends on many factors. It depends on your vision for retirement. What do you want to do in retirement? What level of standard of living do you expect? It depends on your current financial situation and how your plan is structured. It also depends on factors that are out of your control. Think of the inevitable unexpected life events and the unpredictable future economy.

No one can predict the future. However, a fiduciary retirement planner can be the most qualified person to show possible scenarios and options to reduce your risk.

Do I currently have enough savings so that I can retire, or do I need to continue working and saving?

Fiduciary retirement planners have the tools to inform you how much you will need to live the life you want in retirement. Professional planners are trained to know what factors to consider, current and future. They have access to technology and data that can calculate how far off you are from your destination. They can tell you how long it will take to reach your goal under different scenarios. Often, my clients are a lot further along than they think.

Even people who have been conscientious in their financial planning from the get-go have questions. Some are confident they won't run out of money in retirement, but they still need guidance in areas like minimizing taxes and estate planning.

Am I paying more in taxes than I need to? If you are not a tax planner or working with one, the answer to this will likely be yes. Utilizing my team's and my knowledge of the tax code, we can look at the structure of your retirement plan to find strategies that aim to reduce your tax liability. Tax laws are extremely complicated and constantly changing. It's always advisable to seek the advice of a tax planner. Working with one can help to save hundreds of thousands or even millions of dollars over a lifetime.

Clients also ask about how to sustain a healthy portfolio amid an unpredictable financial climate.

Does my portfolio carry too much risk? The answer to this question is not just a matter of future events; the past is relevant here too. Many clients I see have a financial portfolio that was set up in their twenties, thirties, or forties. Unless they have worked with a financial or retirement planner, the structure of that portfolio may never have changed.

That's not a good position to be in. If this is the case, you have a portfolio designed for a twenty-year-old, and if you're closer to sixty, you are likely overexposed. Put simply, if you fear that you have too much risk in your portfolio, you probably do.

The antidote to a poorly balanced portfolio is to rebalance it with less risky options.

What types of investment options are available?

A range of options can build or structure a well-balanced portfolio that is not over-exposed. These options are also good for those approaching retirement. In my opinion, a robust retirement plan will almost always include both market investments and annuities as an option. While many companies focus on just market investments or annuities, it is important to be able to get a perspective from a company that is not limited to just one or the other. People tend to hold certain opinions about annuities, but they are often misguided and can come from investment people who only offer market-based strategies. There are annuities that may be able to enhance your portfolio depending on your situation; you just have to know which ones to use and the pros and cons associated with them.

What are the fees I'm paying for my portfolio?

There's little point in doing your best to plan for sustainable income streams during retirement if much of that income is eaten up by fees. There is also a danger that you may be paying for products that you don't need.

It's wise to spend the time to understand which options are worthwhile and which ones are not worth the fees.

This brings me to the subject of fiduciary retirement planners. Who are they, and how do they differ from non-fiduciaries and financial planners?

In the next chapter, I delve into this. But before I do, understand that financial advisors who are not fiduciaries may recommend financial products that are not the best for you. The products they recommend may benefit them or their affiliation more than options they are not recommending or presenting. These financial advisors can try to sell you something focused more on making them money than benefiting you. That's why working with an independent fiduciary is so critical.

2

WHY YOU NEED A FIDUCIARY RETIREMENT PLANNER

This book answers many questions you may have about retirement planning. However, the most critical point I want to make is why you need a fiduciary retirement planner.

If you are reading this book, you are most likely planning for retirement. You may already also be working with a financial advisor. According to CNBC, close to 40 percent of people over age fifty work with financial advisors. That's not surprising, but what might be is that few of those who claim to be financial advisors (approximately 10–15 percent) are actually fiduciaries.[2]

A fiduciary is legally bound to manage your assets in your best interests. Now, what does that really mean? How does a fiduciary differ from a non-fiduciary retirement planner? What is a financial advisor, and how does a financial advisor compare to a fiduciary or non-fiduciary financial planner? Let's sort out the answers to those questions first.

2　Ryan A. Hughes, "Why You Need to Work with a Fiduciary Financial Advisor," Bull Oak, May 12, 2025, https://bulloak.com/blog/why-you-need-to-work-with-a-fiduciary-financial-advisor/.

What Is a Fiduciary?

A fiduciary is a person held to a fiduciary standard, which means they are obligated to act in their client's best interests. If your advisor is not obligated to act in your best interest, it is time to begin looking for a new financial advisor. I don't believe you should allow someone to manage your life savings who is not held to standards that require them to work in your best interest.

Wealth Managers vs. Retirement Planners

In addition, many financial advisors focus on wealth accumulation. It's fine to work with a wealth manager if you are a young professional or still in your prime working years. At these stages in life, you have plenty of time to take financial risks and recover from them before you retire.

If you plan to retire within the next ten years, it is crucial to work with a fiduciary retirement planner who has specific expertise with retirement strategies.

As you close out your working years, I believe a retirement planner is better for your needs than a wealth manager. This is because you are planning for a specific stage in your life and all that coincides with it. There is a lot more to consider than simply managing stocks, bonds, and other assets.

Fiduciary retirement planners are knowledgeable in planning strategies. They will help you with strategies to replace lost income in retirement. They can help determine the optimal pension option or the optimal time to turn on Social Security. Some can even discuss and suggest Roth conversions that can aim to minimize your tax bill in retirement. Some can let you know how much income you can live on in retirement with a strong probability of success. If your advisor is not suggesting these actions, they are likely not a retirement planner.

Fiduciaries and Non-Fiduciaries

The Consumer Financial Protection Bureau defines a fiduciary as "someone who manages money or property for someone else." A fiduciary accepts that, by law, they must manage their client's assets for their client's benefit. Their primary focus cannot be looking to benefit themselves or their company.

To clarify this, take two financial professionals. One of them is a fiduciary financial advisor and the other is a broker. You might find many similarities.

Both will offer investments. Both will earn some type of fee or commission to manage your investments. Both may have a professional office and a professional team. Both can be charming people and want to develop a strong, personal relationship with you. However, when offering financial recommendations, they are held to two different standards.

Asset Management

Professional number one, the fiduciary financial advisor, must place the client's interests above their own. The fiduciary aims to place the client in a better position for retirement.

The fiduciary may also select strategies that benefit the client but are less beneficial for them or their company.

Fiduciary advisors are also expected to evaluate changes in market conditions. They must consider the effects on investments and interest rates. They must consider a client's risk tolerance to ensure that they are always working in a client's best interest.

Professional number two, the broker, has previously been held to a suitability standard. They were required to make recommendations *suitable* for someone *like* the client. They were not expressly required to put their clients' interests ahead of their own or held to the stringent fiduciary standards of a financial advisor.

This is a key distinction and can be a huge conflict of interest. A broker was previously able to make a recommendation that was *suitable*. However, the client's interests could have been second to those of the broker or their company.

For instance, the broker could have recommended an investment that is less advantageous to the client but still deemed suitable. It might be a strategy that pays the advisor handsomely in return for the recommendation. As of this writing, a law was recently passed requiring brokers to provide recommendations in the client's best interests, but it is not as stringent as the fiduciary standard of a fiduciary retirement planner.

Social Security

A non-fiduciary broker could have advised a client to turn on their Social Security early. This could have been sound advice. There are circumstances where this might be financially prudent for the client. But there may also be a financial incentive for an advisor to give this advice.

If you turn on Social Security early, less money from other investments is required to support your lifestyle. This means you can keep more funds in your brokerage accounts. The broker may bill you according to the amount of assets they manage for you or earn a commission from the amount of money moved in a trade. The more assets you have in your broker-age account, the more the advisor can be paid. Thus, a broker might have an added incentive to encourage you to take Social Security early. The same could be true for a financial advisor who does not do income or Social Security planning as part of the scope of their planning.

In contrast, a fiduciary retirement planner would only recommend turning on Social Security if it is in your best interest. If it is better for you to claim Social Security at seventy, and a fiduciary is evaluating

Social Security for you, then this will be the fiduciary's recommendation.

Tax Planning

Tax planning is another area of differentiation. Tax advice from a fiduciary financial advisor must be in the best interest of the client in mind. The fiduciary who does tax planning will understand a client's tax situation and consider ways to lessen their tax burden.

In contrast, most financial advisors who do not do tax planning and brokers disclose the following:

"XYZ Company does not provide tax advice. Please consult your tax professional."

Not all financial advisors are required to advise you regarding your tax bill. They might, but the advice they give might be—you guessed it—*not* in your best interest.

Working with a fiduciary retirement planner can be advantageous. When deciding between a fiduciary and a non-fiduciary, choose the fiduciary. It is crucial that the person who is working for you is working with your best interest in mind.

Choosing a Retirement Planner

"I have been with my advisor for the past thirty years, and I really like him."

This is a phrase I sometimes hear from new clients. They may be considering working with me specifically or our company for their retirement planning. Yet they already have a trusted advisor. And I get it. The relationship between a financial advisor and a client is privileged and personal.

Most financial advisors and retirement planners I know are good people. They find it easy to connect with people and are fun to be around. People tend to build a solid relationship with their advisor over years or even decades. They have shared life experiences with their advisors.

Some of our closest clients are the ones we have served for over a decade, so we understand the bond that is created. Some people remain with their original advisor even if we suggest a more lucrative path. Fundamentally, not all financial professionals provide the same level of service.

Some financial professionals only work in the brokerage space and only offer brokerage account-specific investments.

Some financial professionals work purely in the insurance space and only offer insurance-specific strategies. While this can be helpful if looking only for an insurance solution, this can be a problem if you are desiring to have a retirement plan completed for you. Many of these financial professionals do not do extensive retirement planning.

Some financial professionals are only knowledgeable in the brokerage space. That means they shouldn't advise you on insurance space. They might refer you to someone in the insurance space. Or in order to manage more of your funds, they can likely steer you toward a potentially inferior brokerage solution.

Another category of financial advisors are investment advisor representatives (IARs). IARs work in the advisory space for a Registered Investment Advisor (RIA) company. These advisors can typically have access to a broader range of investing vehicles than a broker.

However, not all RIA companies are the same either. Some RIA companies still focus primarily on the Assets Under Management (AUM) or the insurance space. Some RIA companies focus specifically on wealth accumulation. Some RIA companies focus on retirement planning.

This gives you some idea of the complex world of financial advising. Here's a distinction between wealth advisors and retirement planners, fiduciary or not.

Whether You Need a Wealth Advisor or a Retirement Planner May Come Down to Age

A wealth advisor may be the best person for you if want to accumulate wealth and are working. A typical client for a wealth advisor would be someone in their twenties, thirties, or forties.

A wealth advisor can help you plan. They can help you save money for a child's education, their wedding, a new car, or a down payment on a home. They can help you budget and manage debt. They can also help with market-based portfolio solutions at a stage in life when you have time to weather any stock market crashes.

Retirement planners focus on a different stage in your life. A retirement planner helps you distribute your wealth. They help you manage your wealth over your pre-retirement and retirement years. Typical clients are between fifty and one hundred years old.

These advisors provide strategies to maximize Social Security, pension, annuity, and investment income. Many of these advisors also understand investments designed for the risk tolerance of mature clients.

Risk tolerance later in life should differ from risk tolerance early in life. In most cases, your exposure to risk should be lower later in life. That's because you do not have time to build back a portfolio following an economic downturn. Also, you will be drawing income from your portfolio when you retire, and your ability to leverage compounding will be less.

Regarding risk, let's say a client only wants to take on half the risk of the market. The retirement advisor could eliminate market risk for half of the investment portfolio. Some retirement advisors also look into estate planning. Estate planning includes a plan for wills, trusts, and powers of attorney. It covers strategies to minimize taxes in retirement, often with the assistance of a tax and/or legal professional.

Retirement planners can advise you as to how much to save into your 401(k) and whether you should save pre-tax or Roth. Some may even go so far as to prepare your taxes for you. Some are insurance licensed and will be able to suggest insurance options—life, long-term-care, home, auto, umbrella, and health plans—based on your needs.

That's a summary of the differences between a wealth advisor and a retirement planner.

There is one last point regarding age, and this addresses the age of the advisor. According to MarketWatch, just 10 percent of financial advisors are age thirty-five or younger. In the future, mature planners will age out of the workforce, leaving a shortage of professionals.

An aged financial professional's experience is valuable, but youth brings another advantage. A young advisor offers the potential of a long-lasting relationship. A younger advisor is not likely to retire and abandon you in the near future. They can bring stability and assurance to the relationship. Is it better to work with one advisor for the long term or three or more advisors over shorter terms? That's for you to decide. I do believe, however, that youth brings longevity and fresh perspectives and initiatives.

Not all financial advisors are financial planners, but all financial planners are financial advisors. There is a key distinction between them. Depending on your stage of life, or your particular needs, any one of these types of advisors might be best for you. This book is for those who are approaching or in retirement. I suggest choosing a fiduciary retirement planner.

How Can I Tell if My Advisor Is a Fiduciary Retirement Planner?

How can you find out if your current advisor is a fiduciary retirement planner? The simplest way is through a Google search.

A Google search will show you how an advisor is designated. For example, an advisor might be listed as a "captured agent." A captured agent is an insurance producer or financial professional who can only work with one company. A captured agent is, by definition, typically not a fiduciary.

Another way to tell? If the person only provides insurance or annuity options from one company, they are not a fiduciary. The company can either be their own or one that they are mandated to use.

For example, a big bank-affiliated advisor or broker dealer could offer a limited range of products. Their products could be those that their company and the affiliated bank allows them to use.

You can also look up an advisor on the Securities and Exchange Commission (SEC) site: https://adviserinfo.sec.gov/.

Type in the person's name or firm in the individual or firm section. Do they work for a broker dealer? If so, they will be listed as a broker. If a broker is working for a broker dealer, they are held to the fiduciary standard at all times. Are they listed as an investment advisor working for an investment advising firm? In this case, they are more likely to be a fiduciary.

If the person claiming to be an advisor is not on the SEC site, they likely are not licensed to sell securities or buy market investments for their clients.

Note that even if the advisor is held to a fiduciary standard, they still may not be a retirement planner. Here's how to find out if a person is a retirement planner. Go to the firm's website and look for the terms "retirement" and "retirement planning." If you do not see these words, it is unlikely that the company focuses on retirement planning.

Here's an insider tip. Ask an advisor what financial planning tools they use. If they say they only use an Excel spreadsheet or a legal pad and a pen, they are not likely a retirement planner, or at least a reliable one.

eMoney, MoneyGuidePro, Right-Capital, and Asset-Mark are the most common financial planning software tools.

If an advisor uses one of these tools and they are listed as an investment advisor on https://adviserinfo.sec.gov/, chances are they are a reliable fiduciary retirement planner.

Lastly, ask them to provide the answers to the retirement questions most important to you.

3

THE FOUNDATIONS OF RETIREMENT PLANNING

You don't go to school to become the best chef in the world right after you graduate. School is always a starting point . . . you go to school to build a foundation, and you want to build a foundation that's not going to crumble.
—Roy Yamaguchi

How you structure your retirement portfolio is highly personal. Everybody's financial situation will be different. That said, there are fundamentals upon which to build a plan. Going into retirement, it is very important to know how much income you will need and how much income you will have among various income sources. Social Security and pensions can be large components of many people's income. Let's take a look at both.

The Social Security Act of 1935

President Roosevelt signed the Social Security Act into law in 1935. This program was a response to the dire circumstances caused by the Great Depression. Initially, Social Security addressed the need to provide some form of economic security for the elderly. Workers paid taxes while employed. In doing so, they contributed to a program that would provide income when they retired at age sixty-five or older. The Act also provided some protection against job loss.

The program did not provide disability coverage and medical benefits at first.

However, it did provide other benefits. These included unemployment insurance, old-age assistance, and aid to dependent children. The program also included grants to the states to provide various forms of medical care.

In 1937, the Post Office began distributing applications for Social Security. It also began assigning the first Social Security numbers (SSNs). Next, the government began to collect taxes under the Federal Insurance Contributions Act (FICA). These taxes were deposited in newly created special trust funds.

According to the Social Security Administration (SSA), more than $8.7 trillion has been paid into the trust funds and more than $7.4 trillion has been paid out in benefits. What's left is currently on reserve in the trust funds and will be used to pay future benefits.[3]

---

3   "Historical Background and Development of Social Security," Social Security Administration, accessed November 9, 2025, https://www.ssa.gov/history/briefhistory3.html.

From 1937 until 1940, Social Security benefits were a single, lump-sum payment. Monthly benefits began in 1942. Initially, the ratio of workers to Social Security beneficiaries was high. The ratio was approximately sixteen workers for every beneficiary.[4] Today, according to Pew Research, there are three workers per beneficiary. This is mostly due to the aging population and longer lifespans. By the end of this century, the ratio is projected to decline to 2.1. There will be 230.7 million workers and 110.4 million people collecting benefits.[5] With more recipients, there are fewer funds, which threatens the sustainability of Social Security.

President Ronald Reagan tried to shore up Social Security funds when he

4   "Strengthening Social Security for Future Generations," *Policies in Focus* under President George W. Bush, The White House, 2005, accessed November 9, 2025, https://georgewbush-whitehouse.archives.gov/infocus/social-security/.

5   Drew Desilver, May 20, 2025. "What the Data Says About Social Security." *Pew Research Center*, May 20, 2025, https://www.pewresearch.org/short-reads/2025/05/20/what-the-data-says-about-social-security/.

signed the Social Security Amendments of 1983 into law. The amendments included a new provision. The provision was to tax benefits up to a maximum of 50 percent for individuals whose incomes exceeded a certain threshold. Then, in 1993, the taxable portion of benefits was increased to 85 percent for higher-income beneficiaries.

Today, Social Security is a hot topic. There is some debate about its sustainability. The SSA website states, "As a result of changes to Social Security enacted in 1983, benefits are now expected to be payable in full on a timely basis until 2037, when the trust fund reserves are projected to become exhausted."[6]

What will happen then? According to the SSA, only 76 percent of benefits may be paid (a reduction of up to 24%) unless changes are instituted. The Board of Trustees has outlined changes that could resolve

6   Stephen C. Goss, "The Future Financial Status of the Social Security Program," *Social Security Bulletin* 70, no. 3 (August 2010), https://www.ssa.gov/policy/docs/ssb/v70n3/v70n3p111.html.

the issue. These could be "an immediate reduction in benefits of about 13 percent, or an immediate increase in the combined payroll tax rate from 12.4 percent to 14.4 percent, or some combination of these changes, would be sufficient to allow full payment of the scheduled benefits for the next seventy-five years." This seems unlikely.

The information indicates that Social Security benefits could be reduced by up to 25 percent per person at some point. You want your retirement plan to work even if this reduction occurs. I will discuss Social Security in more detail, including when to take it, in Chapter 7.

Social Security in Retirement

When you retire, you lose the regular payments that were your salary. Your retirement plan needs to clearly lay out how you will replace your salary when you retire so that you can maintain your standard of living. One way to start getting to that goal is by claiming Social Security benefits.

For instance, let's say your income pre-retirement was $10,000 a month. Let's also say that your Social Security will provide $5,000 and you have a pension that will provide $3,000. In this case, your portfolio should be structured in such a way that it will provide the additional $2,000 every month you will need.

In another example, let's say your Social Security will provide only $3,000 and you are not lucky enough to have a pension. In this case, your portfolio should be structured to provide an additional $7,000 every month.

Let's first take a closer look at Social Security, a core component of retirement income.

You can start collecting Social Security as early as sixty-two or delay taking it until you are seventy. After you reach full retirement age, the Social Security payout amount that you will receive goes up 8 percent per year. Full retirement age varies depending on your date of birth. For most people, it is between the ages of sixty-six and sixty-seven.

The 8 percent increase each year is something to consider when deciding when to take Social Security. If you are likely to live beyond age eighty-one (in most cases), you are better off waiting to turn on Social Security until you are seventy rather than turning it on sooner (ignoring some other factors). That's because after age eighty-one, the additional payments you will have received will compensate for the years when you did not receive payments, and you will continue receiving larger payments.

If you delay taking Social Security, you will need funds in your portfolio to supplement your income. For example, if you want to retire at sixty-five and not seventy, do you have the funds in your portfolio to supplement your income for five years until you can claim benefits?

If the answer is no, you might have to turn on Social Security sooner, even if it makes sense financially to wait until you are seventy.

Social Security Specifics

If you were married for ten years and you haven't remarried, you could file for Social Security benefits based on a former spouse. If your spouse passed away and you're a widow or widower, you could turn on your Social Security based on their Social Security amount as early as age sixty.

There are also benefits for children and parents if one of the parents passes away before the child reaches age seventeen.

One thing to note: There is a cap on how much you can earn if you are receiving Social Security before your full retirement age.

In 2025, if you're under full retirement age, the annual earnings limit is $23,400. If you will reach full retirement age in 2025, the limit on your earnings for the months before full retirement age is

$62,160. Starting with the month you reach full retirement age, there is no limit on how much you can earn and still receive your benefits.[7]

Choosing Pension Options

Few people are lucky enough to have a pension these days. Pensions were largely replaced by retirement savings accounts, such as the 401(k). Companies wanted to reduce their costs, and transferring the risk of retirement savings onto employees was one way to do that. It was expensive to pay employees a pension for the rest of their lives.

In the 1980s, the United States started to phase out pensions as a result of new regulations from the Internal Revenue Service. A new provision was introduced by the 1978 Revenue Act. This provision

---

7   "Receiving Benefits While Working," Social Security Administration, accessed November 9, 2025, https://www.ssa.gov/benefits/retirement/planner/whileworking.html.

allowed people to use pre-tax funds for contributions toward retirement plans.

Around 30 percent of people had a pension (defined benefit plan) in the early 1980s. In 2024, only around 15 percent of people had a pension.

Active Participants in Private-Sector Pension Plans 1975-2019

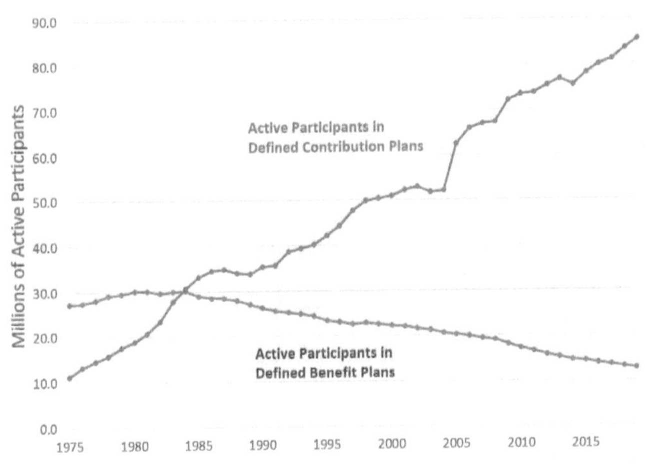

Even the pensions that do still exist may not be as well funded as they previously were.

Employers often bear the heavy responsibility of fully funding pension plans. This is a risky and costly proposition. The economy is characterized by unpredictable market volatility and fluctuating investment returns. Also, managing pension plans is complex. There are government regulations to adhere to. Even then, there is no guarantee that a pension plan will continue to provide promised benefits.

About a year ago, I was meeting with a client who was receiving a pension that paid him around $2,200 every month. My client had received a letter from the pension company. The letter informed him that the company was having issues with its funding and was reducing his monthly payment from around $2,200 a month to approximately $1,000 a month.

It seems shocking that a company can suddenly inform a beneficiary that they will no longer receive promised funds. The payments can disappear or be reduced if the company can no longer guarantee the full amount.

My job was to find a way to replace that shortfall of $1,200 each month from his portfolio so he and his family could maintain their same lifestyle in retirement.

Single-Life, Joint, Survivorship, Period-Certain, and Lump-Sum Pension Options

The range of pension options can be confusing. As a fiduciary retirement planner, I review the options and determine which ones make the most sense for a client and their family.

Single-Life Payout

A pension will usually have a single-life payout, which is the highest dollar amount available from a pension. This option may make sense if you're single and you want to take as much income out from that pension as you can. If you are married or have children, this option may not be the best. That's because if something happens to you, that money passes away with you. The pension will no longer continue to pay out, and there will not be a death benefit that goes to your spouse or other family members.

Joint and Survivorship Options

Some pensions offer a 50 percent or 75 percent joint survivorship option. Here, the income from your pension is guaranteed to go to the surviving spouse. If something happens to you, your spouse will still receive your pension benefits.

If selecting an income option, we usually recommend a 100 percent joint and survivorship option plan. The reason is that if one of the spouses passes away, the Social Security payments for the spouse with the lower-paying Social Security goes away.

For example, take a husband and wife who both have Social Security turned on.

The husband receives $4,000 a month and the wife receives $3,000. If the husband passes away, the wife will lose the $3000 a month in Social Security. She will be left with the husband's payout of $4,000. In essence, the wife loses $3,000 a month of income.

In this scenario, with a single-life payout, the wife would lose both the lower Social Security payment and the pension. Since we want to avoid this unnecessary risk, we would typically recommend the 100 percent survivorship option if taking the income option.

Survivorship options tend to have a lower overall payout than the single-life option. Our clients are usually willing to forgo that extra income to make sure both spouses are covered.

Period-Certain Option

A period-certain option is one that offers a payout for a certain period; it might be for five years, ten years, or fifteen years. Period-certain plans can be for single life or joint life. These plans also have advantages for beneficiaries.

Let's take a ten-year period-certain policy. Let's also say that both spouses pass away one year after receiving income payouts. The remaining payouts will go to a designated beneficiary for the next nine years. Thus, nine years of payments are not completely lost.

Lump-Sum Option

Another option can be to take the income in the form of a lump sum. In this case, you can roll over the funds saved in the pension to an IRA. Unlike keeping them within the pension plan, you can now invest them, manage them, and integrate them into your tax planning.

In some cases where fixed income is still desired, our client can use the lump-sum option to purchase an income annuity. Similar to a pension, an income annuity provides an additional income stream throughout retirement. Here, instead of the income coming from a pension, it will come from the annuity. In some cases, the open market can offer annuities that may be able to pay a higher amount than the pension would.

If you use an annuity instead of a pension, and if you were to pass away early, the money remaining in the annuity would go to your beneficiaries. If your funds were in a pension that was not period certain, you might lose all the money that was saved into the pension.

Let's say you have a 100 percent joint and survivorship option. If you and your spouse both passed away after the first year, that pension money may be gone. None of it would go to your beneficiaries. In contrast, if you had your own income annuity and you turned on the income for one year, all the money remaining in that annuity would go to your beneficiaries.

Pension Tax Planning

If you use your own income annuity, you can have tax-free income later in life because you can convert that annuity into a Roth IRA.

For example, let's say you invest $100,000 in an annuity. For the sake of easy math, let's say the annuity pays out $10,000 a year. Around year nine, there might be $10,000 left. You can Roth-convert that annuity if you started it with IRA dollars.

Let's say you have funds in your 401(k) or your 403(b). A 403(b) is a tax-sheltered annuity (TSA). A TSA is a retirement savings plan available to employees of public schools and certain tax-exempt organizations. Let's also say that you put those funds into an IRA income annuity. Once the value reaches a certain level—$10,000, for example—you only have to pay the taxes on a much smaller amount since you are converting a significantly lower amount than the initial $100,000. That money is now tax-free income.

We restructure retirement plans for our clients to show them how much income they can live on in retirement. In 2024, we were able to show the new people we met with how they could financially afford to live on an average of $26,000 more per year than they were currently spending. That means they could spend over $2,000 per month more than they previously were spending on average after we had restructured their retirement plan.

For example, if a client was currently living on $80,000, we found an additional $26,000 of after-tax income per year for the rest of their lives. This could pay for a trip to Europe or whatever their goals for retirement may be each year!

These financial advantages are achievable. They require taking Social Security at the optimal time and choosing the right pension option. They also require a well-balanced portfolio designed efficiently. We look at a client's ability to aim for top returns, considering their risk tolerance while finding ways to minimize their tax burden.

The Importance of Working with a Fiduciary for Retirement Income Planning

We are fiduciaries, and there are many ways that we put the word "fiduciary" into action. We can be paid less in asset-based management fees by making certain recommendations that put our clients in a better financial position. A practical example is the way that we help our clients select their Social Security.

According to Money.usnews.com, the most common age to turn on Social Security is age sixty-six.[8] Many people turn on their

8   Emily Brandon and Erica Sandberg, "The Most Popular Ages to Collect Social Security," U.S. News, August 14, 2023, https://money.usnews.com/money/retirement/social-security/articles/the-most-popular-ages-to-collect-social-security.

Social Security income in the year they retire. This is often an intuitive decision because they are losing their income from work and want to replace that income with Social Security.

Some financial advisors suggest this strategy. Often, they are advisors who do not use financial planning software or who claim to do not do income planning as part of their advising. This strategy works well financially for some advisors. That's because by drawing down Social Security, less income needs to be taken from the client's portfolio. Thus, there is more money in the client's portfolio. The more money in the portfolio, the bigger the management fees claimed by the advisor.

The decision of when to start drawing on Social Security can present a conflict of interest. If an advisor suggests taking Social Security when the timing is not in the best interest of the client, it is an example of how an advisor might not be working in a client's best interests.

We use financial planning software to make sure that we are acting in a fiduciary capacity for each of our clients. We want to maximize the probability of success for the client. Often, turning on Social Security at age seventy is the best decision for financial planning. When this is the case, we recommend this to our clients despite collecting less in management fees up front by recommending this option.

We also show our clients how to save hundreds of thousands of dollars in taxes in many cases over the course of their lifetimes. One of the ways we do this is by using our financial planning software and our financial planning team to determine the optimum amount to convert from an IRA to a Roth IRA each year.[9]

If a client is still working, we inform

---

9   This is substantiated using our financial planning software and comparing people's current tax planning strategies to our recommended tax planning strategies. In 2023, for the financial plans we created, we were able to show an average of over $500,000 saved in taxes over a person's or a couple's projected financial planning period.

them if they should be saving into their pre-tax or Roth portion of their 401(k)s and other retirement plans. I have yet to come across a client whose advisor recommended precisely how much to convert for the year within their retirement plans and from which funds to pay taxes.

Some advisors offer this service, but I've found the ones that do to be rare. If your advisor is not showing you these tax strategies, they may be limited in terms of what they offer or they are not fiduciary financial advisors. Worse yet, you could unknowingly be paying hundreds of thousands of dollars more in taxes. It's worth consulting with a tax planning professional or a fiduciary retirement planner who offers tax planning as one of their services.

If you are selecting pension options, this is another time to work with a fiduciary.

What if you have the option to take either an income payout or a lump-sum payout from a pension? It is important that your financial advisor uses financial planning software. Sophisticated software will help them to be able to evaluate the two options. The advisor can then make a data-driven recommendation. The client can either turn on the income or roll over the pension.

If you are working with a financial professional who is not a fiduciary, again, there may be a conflict of interest. The advisor would likely benefit if you increase the assets under their management using a rollover.

In my opinion, if the advisor is not using financial planning software, their basis for a recommendation has less merit. It may not be based on the overall financial plan, and it may be based on an opinion or rule of thumb.

We use financial planning software to help determine the best options for our clients. We look at the repercussions of turning on their pension or rolling it over into an IRA. This helps us to work in our fiduciary capacity, limit conflicts of interest, and work in the best interest of the client.

Lastly, if you are selecting investments for your portfolio, it's important to work with a fiduciary. Different investments can mean different pay structures for an advisor. For example, a broker might be paid more if you choose one type of investment or mutual fund over another. This presents a conflict of interest for the advisor.

Let's say you are working with an advisor who offers insurance-based strategies. The advisor might get paid more if you choose a particular insurance company. If the advisor is only held to the suitability standard, they might find an investment that is simply "suitable for someone like you." What you may not be told is that it pays the advisor more. If the advisor were held to the fiduciary standard, they would be obligated to find an investment planning strategy that is in your best interest.

We look for the highest payout and

growth investments for our clients instead of looking for the highest payouts for our company. Regarding an income fixed indexed annuity, we look for the highest income payout from a strongly rated carrier. Then, we will recommend that option to our client.

If we are looking for a growth-based annuity strategy, we look for the highest crediting rates available. We make sure the rate is from a highly rated insurance carrier with a strong renewal history. Then, we make that recommendation to our client.

We are a client-focused company that holds fast to the fiduciary standards of advising. The income an annuity provides can vary significantly based on the strategy selected. The difference between one strategy and another can be enormous. In some cases, it would cost twice the amount to provide the same amount of income per year! Which one you choose matters.

4

BALANCING YOUR PORTFOLIO AS YOU APPROACH RETIREMENT

I've been a cook all my life, but I am still learning to be a good chef. I'm always learning new techniques and improving beyond my own knowledge . . . there is always something new to learn and new horizons to discover.
—Jose Andrés

Think back to those distant days when you were twenty years old. You may have been in college, starting to work, or starting a family. What was important to you then and the risks you were willing to take were very different from your priorities as you approach retirement.

If your attitude toward risk has changed, your investment portfolio should have changed also. If not, then you are not well positioned for retirement. Whether you work with an advisor or manage your investments on your own, your portfolio should reflect your risk threshold. If your portfolio carries the same level of risk as it did decades ago, you might not achieve the goals you have for retirement.

When you are in your twenties, that might be the time to have a high-risk portfolio. When I was twenty years old, I was wrestling Division 1 for Bucknell University. I was grappling and battling against some of the top athletes in the country, risking injury all the time. I would do all-out sprints around the track until the coach thought we had had enough. At that time, I would carry 45-pound plates from the gym to the football stadium and up and down each bleacher, one-armed push-ups, bear crawls around the track, you name it.

Now, I would never risk getting hurt doing these crazy exercises. I learned my lesson a few years ago, after I graduated, when I jumped over a neighbor's fence and cut up my leg in the process. I realized (after the fact) the risk was not worth the reward, and I did not dare to take the same level of risk as I was getting older.

If your portfolio is completely invested in equities and the stock market dips by 48 percent, you may be taking on more risk than you feel comfortable with. During the 2008 global financial crisis, the market dropped by that amount and portfolio values halved.[10]

---

10   Peter Gratton, "Stock Market Crash of 2008," *Investopedia*, updated November 21, 2024, https://www.investopedia.com/articles/economics/09/subprime-market-2008.asp.

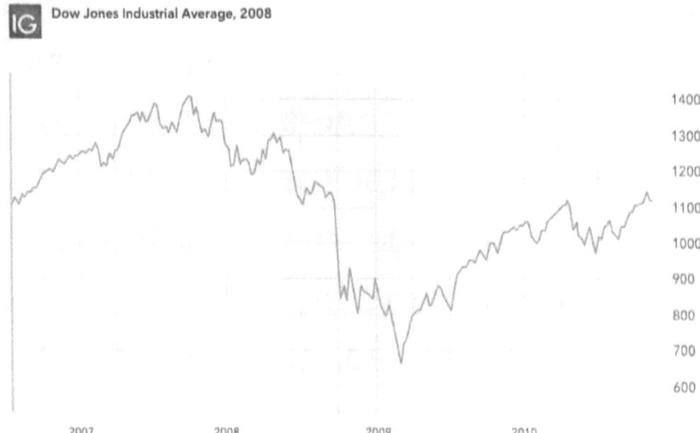

Source: IG Charts[11]

At age twenty, this might not be an issue, since you would have plenty of time to recoup the losses before you retire. However, this could be a problem at age sixty-five if you were looking to retire in the next few years or you just retired.

A crucial change needs to happen as you near retirement, and it could be the difference between retiring sooner rather than later. If the market crashes at the beginning of your retirement, it will take

11   "The Worst Stock Market Crashes of All Time," IG, accessed November 9, 2025, https://www.ig.com/en/ trading-strategies/the-worst-stock-market-crashes-of- all-time-181031.

you some time to recoup your losses. That's why rebalancing is crucial as you age.

In 2008, when the stock market plummeted nearly 50 percent in less than a year, it was devastating for 401(k) and retirement accounts. Have you changed your portfolio to lower your risk as you are approaching your retirement years? If you have not lowered your risk, why haven't you? If you have not lowered your risk and you have a financial advisor, why has your advisor not talked to you about lowering your risk?

Many people do not change their risk because they are either unaware of the need or their advisor does not show them worthwhile strategies. Let's take a look at some strategies that do not have market risk or at least protect your principal.

Risk Mitigation Strategies

Risk mitigation strategies can be subject to low risk or no market risk. They are also expected to receive lower projected rates of returns than higher risk strategies.

No-Market-Risk Strategies
1. Cash or Checking Account

The first of the no-market-risk strategies is a tool you already possess. Cash. Cash carries no market because if the stock market crashes, your cash retains its value. That said, you do lose purchasing power when the price of goods and services go up. Additionally, cash does not give you any potential for return. If you had put $100,000 in a safe in 1985, in 2025, you still had $100,000, and it did not keep up with inflation.

Another no-market-risk tool is your checking account. The funds in your checking account pay your monthly bills. Ideally, your checking account should include one to two months of living expenses to pay your monthly bills.

The majority of checking accounts do

not credit interest for the funds you keep there. The ones that do, typically provide less than 1 percent interest. However, your money is protected by a federal program up to a certain threshold. Thanks to the Federal Deposit Insurance Corporation (FDIC), your money in the bank is insured up to $250,000 per person or $500,000 for a joint account with two people.

2. Savings Account

Your savings account is also a no-market-risk option and is a place to store the majority of your emergency fund, ideally three to six months of living expenses. It's a good idea to keep a larger balance in your savings account than in your checking account because a savings account will typically earn more interest on the balance.

Over the past twenty-five years, the interest rates on savings accounts have been abysmal. More recently, interest rate increases have brought some high-yield savings account interest rates to around 3 percent or more.[12]

3. Certificate of Deposit (CD)

A Certificate of Deposit (CD) is a no-market-risk option often used in tandem with or in lieu of a savings account. CDs offer similar, sometimes slightly higher interest rates than the high-yield savings accounts. Funds kept in a CD are locked up for a period of time (three months, six months, nine months, one year, etc.). During this period, you can take the money out if needed in case of an emergency, but you typically would lose the last three months of interest as a penalty.

4. Fixed Annuity

Fixed annuities, or multi-year guaranteed annuities (MYGAs), offer a fixed interest

---

12 Matthew Goldberg and Karen Bennett, "Best High-Yield Savings Accounts of November 2025 (Up to 4.21%)," Bankrate, updated November 9, 2025, https://www.bankrate.com/banking/savings/best-high-yield-interests-savings-accounts/.

rate for the life of the annuity. In concept, they work like a CD. The annuity has a fixed interest rate that can be expected throughout the life of the term. If the MYGA has a three-year term, then the interest rate will be guaranteed by the insurance company for the full three years. In today's interest rate environment, MYGAs are providing between 4 percent and 5.50 percent for periods between two and twenty years. Some fixed annuities allow you to take a percentage of your funds out each year, and some allow for only interest to be taken. The withdrawal percentages can also vary depending on the annuity. At the end of the term, you will have the option to renew with the same company at the interest rates offered by the company at that time. You can also scan the open market to find a potentially better option.

5. Fixed Indexed Annuity (FIA)

Another no-market-risk strategy is a fixed indexed annuity (FIA). A fixed indexed annuity is different from a fixed annuity. The difference lies in the way interest is calculated and the typical long-term rates of returns. Fixed annuities, or MYGAs, offer a guaranteed, fixed interest rate for a specific period, which gives you predictable interest. FIAs, on the other hand, tie their interest to the performance of a market index, such as the S&P 500, which can give a higher rate of return for the added unpredictability.

Over time, FIAs tend to have more earning potential than other no-market-risk investments. These can vary in terms of how long they can be held, but most surrender charge periods are typically not less than five years or more than fourteen years. Insurance brokers, financial advisors, brokerage firms, and banks may be able to offer FIAs as long as they are properly licensed. You can also get an FIA directly through a provider or life insurance company. When interest rates are lower, the interest credited from an FIA is typically lower. However, in a higher-interest-rate environment, we have seen FIAs earning rates as high as 6–8 percent with top-tier insurance companies.[13]

FIAs offer many of the benefits of the stock market without the more undesirable aspects. Some of the ways interest can be credited to an account are cap rates and participation rates.

With a cap rate, you earn the full interest of the stock market up to a certain point, which is called a cap. Let's say you have a 10 percent cap rate. Let's also say the stock market went up 15 percent from the time you purchased the annuity until the end of the term (one year being the most common term we see). You would earn 10 percent, or the full cap amount, over that period.

In contrast, with a participation rate,

---

13   "Best 5 Year Fixed Annuity Rates for November 2025," My Annuity Store, updated November 9, 2025, https:// myannuitystore.com/annuities/fixed-annuity-rates/5- year/.

you would earn a percentage of the amount that the stock market increased. Let's say you have a 50 percent participation rate. Let's also say the stock market goes up 15 percent from the time you purchase the annuity to the end of the term. It could also be from the end of the previous term to the beginning of the next one. You would earn 7.5 percent over that period. In both circumstances, if the market went down (5, 10, 50 percent, etc.) over that period, the principal would remain the same.

FIAs typically require a time commitment. That time commitment is usually between five and fourteen years. Ten years is the most common period for the ones we have used. The time commitments make an FIA an unfeasible investment for a large sum of money that you would like to withdraw after a short period. These annuities typically offer a free withdrawal provision. The provision allows for an amount (usually up to 10 percent of the account value) to be withdrawn annually without penalty. Not all FIAs are created equal, and there is substantial variability between the top-tier FIAs and the mediocre FIAs. There are also different types of FIAs, such as income FIAs and growth FIAs.

Income FIAs provide an income stream similar to a pension. These annuities benefit someone who is looking for a guaranteed fixed income stream in retirement. They might not have enough income from a pension (if available) and Social Security to support their lifestyle. One of the advantages of this tool is that the income is guaranteed. As long as either the policy owner or their spouse (if a joint option is selected) is still living, they will receive funds depending on the payout option they have chosen.

The starting income date can be in the first year or deferred until income is needed. If the annuitant or owner dies prematurely, the beneficiaries are still left with the account value of the annuity.

There are some disadvantages to this strategy. There are often fees for the income benefit. The funds are not particularly accessible, and it can be difficult to withdraw more than the income amount. Doing so can disrupt the future income amount. Also, the cap and participation rates are usually noticeably lower for these annuities compared to the growth FIAs.

A growth FIA would benefit people whose Social Security and pension are satisfying their income needs. These people do not need a guaranteed income stream. Growth FIAs typically have higher caps and participation rates than income FIAs. According to The Annuity Expert, top-tier growth FIAs have averaged 5–7 percent returns over the past twenty-five years.[14]

Growth FIAs have some advantages.

---

14 Shawn Plummer, "Learn the Average Return on Annuities Before You Buy," *The Annuity Expert*, July 4, 2023, https://www.annuityexpertadvice.com/the-average-return-on-annuities.

They tend to have better growth potential than other no-market-risk strategies. For example, we have historically seen these having better growth potential than the bond market without the interest rate risk, and they usually have no fees attached.

Growth FIAs also have disadvantages. You cannot usually withdraw more than 10 percent of the account value without penalty. The original cap and participation rates may not be fixed for the life of the annuity. Also, the surrender value is not always a fixed percentage and can change along with bonus recapturing (if applicable) and market value adjustments (if applicable).

It's worthwhile to compare the safety of insurance companies with banks. Examine the cash reserves each are required to maintain by their governmental authorities. Typically, a bank is required to keep 8–10 cents per dollar invested with them while the requirements are significantly higher for insurance companies (closer to a dollar for dollar amount is required). This can help explain why it is so rare for insurance companies to fail.

Let's also consider insurance for these companies. Banks are backed by FDIC insurance up to $250,000 per account owner. Insurance companies are also backed at least up to $250,000 per account owner by state nonprofit guaranty organizations. These organizations act like insurance companies for insurance companies.[15] Some states can even offer up to $500,000 per account owner as well.

Although these strategies are safe when looking at the risks, not all annuities, even growth or income annuities, are created equal. There are currently income FIAs with high payout rates and income FIAs with poor payout rates. Similarly, some growth FIAs exist with high caps and

---

15   Patrick Villanova, "Are Annuities Insured?" *SmartAsset*, March 27, 2025, https://smartasset.com/retirement/are-annuities-insured.

participation rates and others with low caps and participation rates. This is why it is important to consult an independent fiduciary retirement planner who can help you find the FIA that works best for you and your retirement plan.

Disclosure: Annuities are designed to be long-term strategies and can involve surrender charges. Early withdrawals may impact annuity cash values and death benefits. For taxable accounts, taxes are payable upon withdrawal of funds. An additional 10 percent IRS penalty may apply to withdrawals prior to age fifty-nine and a half. Annuities are not guaranteed by the FDIC or any other governmental agency and are not deposits or other obligations of or guaranteed or endorsed by any bank or savings association. Guarantees are based on the claims paying ability of the issuing insurance company.

Real Estate Is Not a Low-Risk Option

Real estate investments are risky. Some companies offer real estate investments with a guarantee of a return, but the return is only as strong as the guarantee of that company. The Financial Industry Regulatory Authority (FINRA) is an independent, nongovernmental organization. It protects investors from fraud and bad practices. The body enforces rules governing registered brokers and broker dealers. The SEC is a federal agency that regulates the securities markets and protects investors. These private real estate investments are not regulated by the SEC and may not be held to the same level of scrutiny to protect the consumer.

If you keep a small portion of your money in this type of investment, it might not be a problem, but if you have the bulk of your money invested in this type of company and the company starts to have problems, you could lose much of your investment.

This is not a level of risk someone thinks they may be taking when investing in an investment like this, but it can derail their retirement if they are overexposed and have all their eggs in this basket.

Low-Risk Strategies
1. Bonds

Bonds are considered low-risk investments, and you might expect them to be free of market risk. However, this is not the case, simply because the principal in bonds is not protected. When interest rates increase, the value of bonds decreases. Therefore, if a bond is not held until maturity, you risk losing your principal in your investment.

Many advisors and broker dealers, tend to use bonds as a "less risky" alternative to the equity market. From one aspect, such as a company bankruptcy, they are less risky than the stock market. This is because the company is obligated to pay back the bond holders before they pay back the stockholders.

From other aspects, the bond market can have similar levels or even more downside than the stock market. The common benchmark for the stock market is the S&P 500 Index, and the common benchmark for the bond market is the US Aggregate Bond Index.

In 2022, the SPDR S&P 500 ETF Trust, an exchange-traded fund (ETF) tied to the S&P 500, or SPY (its ticker symbol), went down 18.17 percent. The AGG, or the Bloomberg Aggregate Bond Index used by bond funds as a benchmark to measure their relative performance, went down 13.02 percent.

In 2023, the SPY recovered from its losses with a 26.19 percent gain while the AGG only recovered less than half of its losses with an increase of approximately 5.65 percent. Then, in 2024, the SPY had another year where it returned greater than 20 percent. It reached new all-time highs while the AGG had a return of just 1.31 percent, leaving it at levels still lower than before the 2022 decrease. For this reason, bonds should not be classified as a no-market-risk investment.

Many 401(k) target-date funds are bond heavy. This is particularly the case for those that are approaching maturity. If your 401(k) has a target retirement of 2030 as its primary investment, you likely have a significant amount of your 401(k) invested in bonds.

2. Target-Date Funds (TDFs)

Target-date funds are a popular item in retirement accounts, and they have been increasing in popularity.

According to CNBC, quoting data from the trade group Plan Sponsor Council of America, over 29 percent of retirement account wealth is invested in target-date retirement funds.[16] According to Morningstar, this was close to $4 trillion in 2024.[17]

That number is only expected to increase. CNBC also reported that according to estimates by Cerulli Associates, target-date funds will capture roughly 66 percent of all 401(k) contributions, and about 46 percent of total 401(k) assets will be in TDFs by 2027.

A TDF is a long-term investment account that is automatically adjusted over the years as the investor approaches a specific milestone such as retirement. Early on, TDFs invest more heavily in riskier growth stocks in the market. The idea is that the fund holder has time to recoup any short-term market losses. As time goes

16 Greg Iacurci, "Target-Date Funds—The Most Popular 401(k) Plan Investment—Don't Work For Everyone," *CNBC*, January 6, 2025, https://www.cnbc.com/2025/01/06/are-target-date-funds-the-most-popular-401k-investment-right-for-you.html.

17 "2025 Target-Date Fund Investment Strategy," Morningstar, accessed November 9, 2025, https://www.morningstar.com/business/insights/research/tdf-landscape.

by, the fund investments are rebalanced and become more balanced—for example, fewer stocks and more bonds. This strategy reduces the risk of short-term equity losses as the fund holder approaches retirement.

The rebalancing takes into account when the fund holder plans to retire, which is around the year that appears in the fund name. An example of a TDF is the Fidelity Freedom® 2055 Fund (FDEEX). These funds would be rebalanced at regular intervals to ensure that the fund holders have less market risk as the year of retirement (2055) approaches.

TDFs are becoming more popular because an increasing number of employers are using them as investments for employee 401(k) plans. They are popular among investors who want to "set and forget" their savings. This type of investor prefers a strategy they don't have to worry about rebalancing or making changes to as they age. TDFs can also help active investors who tend to watch the markets and make decisions based on emotions. Watching the markets and reacting can lead to buying high and selling low, eroding portfolio returns.

Drawbacks to Low-Risk TDFs and Bonds

TDFs don't suit everyone, and we usually advise against them when we see them in portfolios. Just because some investors choose the same year to retire, does not mean they should have the same invest-ments. Some might want more risk in their retirement portfolio, and a TDF might not be aggressive enough. Also, the target date of the fund may not give an accurate idea of its risk. A fund with a target data of 2030 is not necessarily a conservative or even a moderate investment. Some of these funds could have up to 60 percent in equities if the date is five years away.

Another drawback of TDFs is their exposure to bonds. While TDFs aim to mitigate risk as you age and get closer to retirement, they aren't the best tools for reducing risk.

To reduce risk as one gets closer to retirement, these TDFs purchase more and more bonds in the portfolio. This would not be as much of a problem in an economic scenario where interest rates are coming down, but that's not always the case and has not been the case in recent years.

Many people do not understand the relationship that bonds have to interest rates. This is an inverse relationship, which means when interest rates go up, the value of bonds goes down; when interest rates go down, the value of bonds goes up.

Here's why this happens. All bonds, whether they are from the government or from a company, are issued at $1,000. Let's say we buy a bond from ABC Company for

$1,000, and it is paying a 4% interest rate over a thirty-year period. Let's also say that, in the next year, the interest rates go up. Now, ABC Company is issuing a new round of bonds for a thirty-year period paying a 6 percent interest rate for $1,000. Is someone still going to pay you $1,000 for your bond that is only paying 4 percent? Not a chance! They could use that same money and purchase a bond for the same period with the same company and get a 2 percent higher interest rate.

Due to this phenomenon, the value of your bond would no longer be $1,000; it would be less. Contrarily, if interest rates went down, the inverse would be true. So, bonds present a challenge if you are unsure in which direction interest rates are going to go. You have a certain level of exposure to your principal.

This is particularly the case for a bond mutual fund, target-date fund, or bond ETF. For instance, in 2022, the stock market went down 18 percent, and the bond market went down 13 percent. If your portfolio was split between both, neither asset protected your principal. Additionally, in 2023, the stock market made a full recovery with 26 percent growth, while the bond market had gone up less than 6 percent, still finding itself in a hole. If you had funds in a strategy that did not go down due to interest rates or stock market losses, you would have had more protection.

5

TAX PLANNING

Balance is key in cooking—you want a little acid, a little sweet, a little savory— the flavors should be harmonious.
—Gail Simmons

A significant portion of retiree wealth is in pre-tax accounts such as traditional IRAs and traditional 401(k)s.[18] I don't believe leaving these funds there is the best plan. When I give presentations on tax planning, I like to refer to this type of tax planning as

---

18 John Wagonner, "How Much Money Do You Need to Retire?," *AARP*, September 12, 2025, https://www.aarp. org/money/retirement/how-much-money-do-you- need-to-retire.html.

"Uncle Sam's tax plan" because it benefits Uncle Sam often to your detriment.

Uncle Sam's tax plan looks like this: People paying into retirement plans receive a deduction for the year that they contribute savings. The required minimum distribution (RMD) age depends on your birth year. The age is seventy-three for people born in 1959 and earlier and seventy-five for people born in 1960 and later. When they hit the minimum age, retirees are forced to start withdrawing money from their IRAs and their 401(k).

This suits your silent partner in retirement, Uncle Sam. The government receives a good chunk of your withdrawals, as you must pay tax on the withdrawals. What's more, when planning for retirement, many people assume that they will be in a lower tax bracket when they retire. They believe that because they are no longer earning money from work, their tax burden will be lower. While this may be the case for some, many people find themselves in a higher tax bracket when they retire.

After you hit your RMD age, the percentage you must withdraw from IRAs (and 401(k)s if you are no longer working) increases each year. Thus, your silent partner, Uncle Sam, takes more each year until you eventually pass away. But taxes are even more complex when you factor in your estate, and they can even go up after you pass away.

Let's say you have a spouse to whom you want to transition your estate when you pass away. Your spouse's tax situation can suffer. Before you passed, you filed jointly as a couple and had a larger tax bracket. The year after you pass away, your spouse's tax bracket changes, as they are now filing as a single person. For example, let's say your income was $80,000 when you were living. You would be in the 12 percent tax bracket as married filing jointly in 2025. Having the same $80,000 in income with a smaller tax bracket means your spouse will have to pay more money in taxes on the same amount of income because they would then be in the 22 percent tax bracket as a single filer.

In effect, the surviving spouse is penalized for their deceased spouse having money in a 401(k) or IRA. The percentage they have to take out per year also continues to rise each year as well. The problem does not stop there. The next beneficiaries of that money are typically the children. The children historically are in their forties, fifties, or sixties and are at the height of their careers and earning potential when they inherit these funds.

When they become the beneficiaries of their parents' estate, they are required to withdraw the funds annually and liquidate the full account within a ten-year period. When they do withdraw the funds, you guessed it, they must pay Uncle Sam, their silent partner. So over the ten years that they are required to withdraw the funds, they might find themselves in a higher tax bracket. This is because of the additional income and having to pay more in taxes.

In short, Uncle Sam's tax plan works really well for the government, but it's not designed to work well for you. That's why it is crucial to have your own personalized income tax plan and a personalized retirement tax plan.

So, what are some of the strategies you can use to mitigate these tax complexities? Roth conversions can be extremely effective here.

Roth IRAs and Tax Planning

The goal of tax planning is to pay the least amount in taxes to Uncle Sam that you can. Of course, you must pay what you owe, but there's no requirement to give him a tip. One strategy we recommend is non-qualified tax deferral strategy. We also call this a non-qualified long-term capital gain strategy.

Money can be saved in a non-qualified

account. A non-qualified account, simply speaking, contains bank funds or after-tax brokerage funds, money earned and saved in the bank and then invested later.

The funds might be later invested in a market-based account that holds a position in stocks, mutual funds, or ETFs. If these funds are held longer than one year, they are subject to capital gains tax treatment instead of ordinary income tax treatment. The long-term capital gains tax treatment can be significantly lower than ordinary tax treatment.

For example, ordinary tax treatment for a married couple with around $200,000 in annual income is around 22 percent. For a married couple in a long-term capital gains tax bracket, the tax rate is only 15 percent. For a married couple making $70,000, the tax rate is 12 percent, and the long-term capital gains tax bracket is 0 percent. So, long-term capital gains treatment can be a way to lower taxes.

Capital Gains Tax Rates in 2025

The long-term capital gains tax bracket rates range from zero to roughly $97,000 taxed at 0 percent for married individuals. Paying long-term capital gains tax rates is one strategy we use to help our clients pay less tax. However, which accounts are used to actually pay those taxes is also a component of tax planning.

2025 Capital Gains Tax Rates and Brackets (Long-Term Capital Gains)
Long-term capital gains face different brackets and rates than ordinary income. The table below shows the tax rates and brackets for 2025.

	For Unmarried Individuals, Taxable Income Over	For Married Individuals Filing Joint Returns, Taxable Income Over	For Heads of Households, Taxable Income Over
0%	$0	$0	$0
15%	$48,350	$96,700	$64,750
20%	$533,400	$600,050	$566,700

Source: Internal Revenue Service, "Revenue Procedure 2024-40."[19]

When you are looking to begin taking money in retirement, we would typically recommend first using money from your non-qualified accounts, IRAs, or 401(k)s. The last account to pull from is a Roth IRA. That's because we want to let the tax-free money in a Roth IRA grow tax-free as long as possible throughout the course of a client's retirement to minimize their RMDs and maximize their tax-free legacy.

---

19   Internal Revenue Service, *Revenue Procedure 2024-40*, accessed November 9, 2025, https://www.irs.gov/pub/irs-drop/rp-24-40.pdf.

Roth Conversions and Retirement Planning

In Chapter 3, I discussed Roth-converting an annuity that is paying an income stream. You can also Roth-convert money invested in a 401(k) or IRA as long as it is a traditional or rollover IRA.

How much should you convert every year to minimize your tax burden?

To answer that question, we rely on financial planning software and our financial planning team to determine the optimal amount. The software allows us to see the effect of various scenarios—converting $50,000, $100,000, $200,000, etc. The software will inform us of the optimal amount for your retirement and the number of years in which you should convert funds. It will also tell us whether it makes sense at all to convert funds or just a small amount depending on your specific circumstances.

Many people ask me, "Why do Roth conversions? Does it really matter whether you pay the tax now or later because the taxes must be paid regardless?" The answer is that it absolutely makes a difference. Let's say, for the sake of easy numbers, you have $100,000 in an IRA or 401(k) that you are not going to touch for the foreseeable future.

This is $100,000 that you are putting aside to spend in five, ten, twenty, or more years. Based on the Rule of 72, we can estimate how long it will take for that amount to double, given a certain interest rate.

The Rule of 72 states that $1 invested at an annual fixed interest rate of 10 percent would take 7.2 years (72 ÷ 10 = 7.2) to double or grow to $2.[20]

---

20 Caroline Banton, "The Rule of 72: What It Is and How to Use It in Investing," *Investopedia*, April 23, 2025, https://www.investopedia.com/ask/answers/what-is-the-rule-72/.

Based on the Rule of 72, if you can get a 6 percent rate of return, that money will double in twelve years. If you can get an 8 percent rate of return, that money will double in nine years. So, in nine to twelve years, your $100,000 investment can double to $200,000. In another nine to twelve years, it can double again, in essence, quadrupling from $100,000 to $400,000 in eighteen to twenty-four years.

Now, if that money is in your 401(k) or IRA, it's taxable. You must make RMDs and pay taxes on those withdrawals. If you had that same $100,000 that you started with and we did a Roth conversion, you have to pay the taxes on it to do the conversion. Let's say you're paying 20 percent in taxes; you can use outside bank accounts to pay those taxes so that the $100,000 stays in that account. Over the same eighteen to twenty-four years, you get the same growth. Assuming it's the same investment, it grows to $400,000, and now you have $400,000 of tax-free dollars instead of $400,000 of taxable dollars.

When you take that money out later in your retirement, you do not have to pay the taxes. If you never touch that money and leave it to your spouse or your children, they do not have to pay the taxes on it either and can take it out tax-free. Additionally, there are no RMDs for Roth IRAs.

In summary, if you don't need the funds, you can let the account continue to grow tax-free, and you don't have to withdraw any of it to satisfy Uncle Sam's RMDs. Roth conversions are a way to pay less taxes in your retirement. You can transition your estate more tax efficiently and more tax-free for the next generation.

Doing a Roth conversion is not complicated, but what can be complicated is figuring out exactly how much to convert and over how many years.

Let's say you have a million dollars saved in your 401(k). You can convert all one million dollars this year into a Roth IRA, but you have to pay the taxes on everything that you convert that year. After the conversion, you will have bumped yourself up to the 37 percent tax bracket. Now you could be paying close to $370,000 in taxes because of the million-dollar conversion you made. So, it doesn't usually make sense to do all the conversions in one year. It also likely will not make sense to convert $50,000 a year for twenty years starting when you are sixty. That's because by the twentieth year, when you're in your retirement, you're converting money when you are eighty years old. There's usually a ten-to-sixteen-year break-even period on that conversion, so now it's taking you too long. You'd likely have to live past ninety years old just to break even.

Again, it's advisable to work with somebody who has the appropriate financial planning software. An equipped tax planner can calculate the optimal amount to convert over those three, five, seven, or ten years that may be best to do the Roth conversions.

I have some clients who are computer engineers and want to use Excel spreadsheets to calculate conversions. An Excel spreadsheet typically will not accurately portray everything you need. Advanced software takes into account factors like changes in tax law and cost of living adjustments. It will integrate the effects of increases in your Social Security or pension income. It will also consider how much you will pay in taxes and more. These are all factors that affect the conversion amount, and they often do not show up on the Excel spreadsheet.

In 2024, we were able to show new people who came in how they could save over $800,000 projected in taxes over the course of their lifetimes. This is an immense benefit of doing proper tax planning!

A few years ago, I had a new client who

had an accountant he had been working with for twenty or thirty years. I met with the accountant to discuss Roth conversions for our mutual client.

"I don't like the idea of Roth conversions," he told me. "Tax planning 101, never pay more in taxes than you have to."

"Well, that's exactly why we *do* Roth conversions," I told him. "If you don't do Roth conversions, when the client turns seventy-three or seventy-five, they have to start taking money out of their IRAs. Those have been growing for several decades. At that point, they're stuck paying a significant amount more than they would need to if they were to do the Roth conversions."

The accountant was only focusing on the client's tax return for this year, and he was not considering what would happen ten years or twenty years in the future. We, however, set up a portfolio for the years and decades to come, rather than just showing how we can try to save money today.

6

LEGACY AND FAMILY IN RETIREMENT PLANNING

Cooking is the ultimate giving.
—Jamie Oliver

What is your vision of a successful retirement? What do you want to do in retirement? What level of quality of living do you expect? What will bring fulfillment for you and those around you when you retire? When you retire, you will have thirty to fifty hours per week to take back your time and do the things that maybe you haven't been able to do while working. And so, we want you to think about what does that look like? These are important questions to ask yourself when you are planning for retirement.

For many people, work takes precedence for most of their lives, and they give little thought to retirement until it is upon them. Many people don't plan well in advance for this important time in their lives.

Besides not planning early enough, it is sometimes the case that one spouse manages the financial planning. We can refer to them as the financial spouse. The other spouse we can refer to as the nonfinancial spouse. In such a case, the financial spouse has the vision for how the finances are going to look. Meanwhile, the nonfinancial spouse may have ideas and a vision that the financial spouse is unaware of.

Working with a retirement planner is an opportunity to bring both spouses into the conversation. We make sure they are both on the same page and aware of how the finances are structured.

The structure of the retirement plan is just one component that spouses need to work together on. Another is the legacy plan. What are the goals regarding estate planning and beneficiaries? What are the goals regarding the heirs or the children?

Some of our clients want to leave a specific dollar amount to each of their kids. Others feel that they have raised their children, paid for their college, paid for their wedding, etc., and that the children are now set. Their children may well be earning more than their parents at this stage. Also, the parents may feel that they do not need to leave them a substantial legacy. The children will receive whatever is left over and be fine.

Other people know that they are going to leave a lot of money, and they want to know how to do that efficiently for tax purposes. They want to leave their legacy as smoothly as they can for the next generation.

Estate Planning

Sound estate planning typically requires setting up wills. It might require setting up trusts that may incorporate home ownership. Estate planning might mean leaving a living legacy. A living legacy allows you to spend the money with your kids and/or gifting the funds to your kids now. That way you can all experience the enjoyment of it together while you are still living rather than when you are gone. Additionally, they will be able to cherish those memories or purchases long after you are gone.

If you finance a family trip or pay for college, a home, or a wedding, your heirs will appreciate it. Why not gift sooner rather than later if you are confident you will not run out of money?

My dad tells a story about a married couple who were looking for help with their financial planning. We hold a discovery meeting for people so we can meet and understand their retirement goals. During the discovery meeting, my dad asked them what they envisioned for retirement.

"I always wanted to live in Florida," the wife said.

The husband looked at her in shock.

"We've been married for forty years, and you've never told me once that you wanted to live in Florida."

After a discussion, the husband said,

"Wow! Okay. That's a lot to take in. I didn't know that."

The couple scheduled a meeting with my dad the following week. A few days before, they called to say that they would need to reschedule the meeting because they were in Florida looking at homes.

The conversation during the discovery meeting was enlightening. In fact, it caused the couple to completely restructure their retirement plan. They took immediate action and went house hunting. They have been living in Florida for twenty years.

We find that in most families where

they manage their own investments, it's common for one spouse to manage the finances. The other spouse often does not have the knowledge or the desire to manage investments in the same capacity. This can be a problem if the financially inclined spouse predeceases the nonfinancial spouse.

If the couple partners with a financial advisor and both spouses are involved, there is a team dynamic. If the financially inclined spouse is unavailable, the nonfinancial spouse is not alone. They have someone who is qualified and knows them who can help them weigh their options and make financial decisions.

If there is no advisor, it's easy for a spouse who has not been involved in the investing to make the wrong decisions. Also, shopping for a financial advisor during a time of grief can be overwhelming and challenging. This is another reason to have a good working relationship built on trust with a financial advisor. It applies even if you have historically managed investments on your own.

7

THE RETIREMENT PLANNING PROCESS

When you retire, I like to say it is as if every day is Saturday and now *you* get to decide how you're going to spend it. It's a good idea to decide how you want to spend your retirement while you're still working. If you don't, you could end up in a position where you are confused or even unhappy at the start of your retirement. This can happen if you have nothing to do in retirement, and you could wind up feeling bored or unsure of what to do.

Retirement is an active choice and lifestyle, so if you are going to retire at some point in your future, it is important to plan for it. Many people spend several hours, days, or even weeks planning a dream vacation. Your dream vacation may only last a few weeks to a few months. Your retirement, if done properly, could last you ten, twenty, thirty, or even more *years*. It is crucial to plan properly so you can enjoy your retirement without having to worry or stress as much as if you had not planned at all.

Another challenge I have seen when it comes to preparing for retirement is the need to switch from a mindset of saving to a mindset of spending. Many people who are close to retiring or have already retired are determined to save money. Since they were young, they have been told to save. Most have done an excellent job of saving thanks to this mindset. However, as they transition from working to retiring, the mindset needs to change from saving to spending. This will help them get the most out of their money and to experience enjoyment and fulfillment in retirement.

Many people I meet with tell me they don't plan to leave any money to their children. I explain to them that by spending what they are currently spending, they can expect to leave millions of dollars to their children. After explaining this, I inform them that they can live on more income than they have been used to. By breaking down the years of saving and transitioning from a saving mindset to more of a spending mindset, they can see how to live to their fullest and get the most out of their savings.

Another challenge I see across the financial industry lies with the age of financial advisors. Many are currently busy planning their own retirements. According to a study done by Cerulli Associates, the average age of a financial advisor is fifty-six years old.[21]

Also, according to a survey conducted by J.D. Power in 2023, 20 percent, or one in five advisors, say they are five years or fewer away from retirement.[22] This means that many people will have to transition from one advisor to another or begin self-management. They may have had a good relationship with an advisor for years or even decades. Now, they must start brand new with someone with whom they may have no history.

In essence, if your current advisor is close to your age or older than you are, you likely will not stay with that advisor throughout your retirement.

21   "The Financial Advisor Industry Has a Headcount Problem," Cerulli Associates, January 16, 2024, https://www.cerulli.com/press-releases/the-financial-advisor-industry-has-a-headcount-problem.

22   "Time-Starved U.S. Financial Advisors Considering Alternative Options," J.D. Power, July 5, 2023, https://www.jdpower.com/sites/default/files/file/2023-06/2023067%20U.S.%20Finanical%20Advisor.pdf.

If any of my clients believe that they would be financially better off with another advisor, then I would want them to work with that advisor. In 2024, we had over a 95 percent client retention rate. Over 95 percent of the clients that were with us at the beginning of the year stayed with us through the end of the year. I am proud that most of our clients wished to continue working with us. If you are on the fence about working with your current advisor or their company, it is likely time to start looking for another advisor. If you don't feel you are in the best position and feel that there is a better way out there, you are probably right.

The Retirement Process

We like to give our clients an idea of what working with us looks like. We follow a process with our clients that we have finely tuned over the years. It starts with establishing a clear picture of how you would like your retirement to look.

1. Getting a Clear Picture

For the relationship between us and our clients to be a successful one, there must be a desire to work toward the same goals. And we do everything we can to nurture a relationship of trust.

Our office is warm and welcoming. We have coffee and fresh-baked cookies. We want to have a casual conversation and simply get to know you. In turn, we want our clients to get to know us. Our clients have often read about us in one of our books. They might have heard about us on the radio. They may have attended one of our workshops. That's great. But if they are entrusting us to guide them to retirement, we want them to trust us as they would their own family or, in some cases, more.

We also offer virtual options for meetings to accommodate clients who are not local or have difficulty coming to the office in person.

Establishing trust is key because in order to best serve you, we have to understand you. We do this by asking lots of questions. We need to know what you want to accomplish in retirement. We need to know the level of market risk that you feel comfortable with. Nobody wants to take any risk, of course. Nobody ever wants to lose money. But if you don't take any risk and you have no market exposure, your rate of return can be far less than what you want or need to accomplish your goals. We work together to find a suitable balance that works best for you.

Your Financial Questionnaire and Risk Tolerance

We gather a great deal of the information we need prior to our first real planning meeting with a client. We hold a discovery meeting during which we ask potential clients to complete a Financial Questionnaire. (See the Appendix for the full questionnaire.)

The Financial Questionnaire helps us to assess where our clients are on the retirement planning journey. It is also important for us to determine a client's risk tolerance.

Your risk tolerance is part of what we use to create your portfolio. Everybody's risk tolerance is different. The assets you have in your portfolio affect your return on investment as they react to the inevitable ups and downs of the stock market.

To find out your risk tolerance, we might ask you to consider the 2008 market crash when the market dropped by close to 50 percent. We ask you how much you could tolerate your portfolio going down if the market dropped by that amount. Would you be comfortable losing 50 percent of your savings? Most people closing in on or in their retirement stage of life would not be comfortable with that loss. So often, we find that number to be 15–35 percent, but it can vary.

Once we understand your risk tolerance, we can look at the investments you have. Do your investments reflect your level of risk tolerance? Do you have too much risk in the portfolio? Do you have too little to give you the returns you need to keep up with inflation?

We also ask our clients to bring in their tax returns so we can better understand their tax situation. If you have an advisor and they are not looking into your tax situation, there can be a huge disconnect between the investment side of things and the tax planning. We also look at our clients' life insurance and estate plans.

We do a thorough calculation using the latest financial planning tools to determine how much income could be provided for retirement. We look at how much has been saved for retirement, pension options, and Social Security.

We will incorporate rental properties. We look at the value of those properties. We look at the value of your home and whether you are looking to downsize. We make sure that we cover everything we need to help create your personalized plan for your retirement.

Creating Your Income Plan for Retirement

There is one overriding financial challenge you will face at retirement: transitioning away from a stable income or paycheck that fills up the bank account every two weeks or every month. To maintain your standard of living in retirement, you must have alternative streams of income.

One of the most common fears of retirees is that they will not have enough income and will run out of money. That said, one of the greatest services we provide our clients is financial peace of mind. We can show them how their various investments can be sufficient to upkeep, or even elevate, their current standard of living. And that is something our clients love to hear!

When to Take Social Security

Social Security used to be something you could rely on and plan for. However, there is now quite a bit of uncertainty surrounding Social Security.

As I mentioned in Chapter 3, Social Security is under threat. According to a report by the trustees of the Social Security and Medicare trust funds, "the Social Security fund will run dry in 2033, unless Congress combines the program's old-age and disability funds, in which case insolvency would arrive in 2034."[23]

What happens then? My personal opinion on this is that we do not have a lot of time until something needs to change here. If the government says they will not have

---

23 "Treasury Releases Social Security and Medicare Trustees Reports," US Department of the Treasury, June 18, 2025, https://home.treasury.gov/news/press-releases/sb0170.

the funding, and they are doing nothing to change that, something is going to have to give. I do believe that Social Security will be modified in some way in order to keep the system. It may come in the way of cutting benefits, increasing taxes on the working class, increasing taxes overall, or a combination of these. In any case, something will need to be done, and we may not be able to rely on the full amount of Social Security income being paid in our retirement.

So if you are currently receiving $4,000 per month, that could go down to around $3,000 per month if the benefits are cut by 25 percent. Although this is not set in stone, it is something that is important to plan for. If Social Security is reduced, how will you make up that shortfall in your post-retirement income? That's one area where a fiduciary retirement planner may be able to help.

They can advise on the timing of Social Security. When to start claiming benefits depends on a few factors. For some people, it might be as soon as they are eligible. For others, the best time could be at full retirement age or later. How do we know? We use sophisticated financial planning software to answer that question.

Also, just because you might decide to delay taking Social Security, that does not mean you must delay retirement. We analyze if you have the funds to bridge the gap between the time when you retire and the time you start to draw Social Security.

A fundamental component of the Social Security calculation is your life expectancy. If you expect to live past age eighty-one (generally speaking), you typically benefit the most by turning on Social Security at age seventy. If you don't expect to live past age eighty-one, you benefit the most by turning it on sooner than age seventy. Of course, no one can predict their own mortality, but we can plan based on the knowledge we do have of our health, the longevity of our parents, and certain advancements in science and medicine.

I talked about collecting Social Security based on a spouse's funds. Basically, you can collect up to one-half of your spouse's Social Security when you reach full retirement age as long as your spouse has already filed for their benefit. Additionally, if your spouse passed away before collecting, you can turn on your deceased spouse's Social Security benefit as early as age sixty. In some cases, you can also then defer your own Social Security until age seventy if it is prudent to do so.

If you were previously married, did not remarry, and you were married over ten years, you can collect on your former spouse's Social Security.

There are many different options when it comes to taking Social Security.

That's why it's best to consult a fiduciary retirement planner. They can help you determine the right time for you to turn on Social Security as well as the pros and cons of the different options. This is because they will be able to know and understand your full financial picture, whereas someone working for Social Security likely will not.

A Tax Planning Myth

We talked about tax planning in Chapter 5. I would like to dispel a popular myth that some people mistakenly subscribe to: *in retirement, you will fall into a lower tax bracket because you are no longer working and earning a salary.*

From our experience with our clients, that is not usually the case. When our clients retire, they want to maintain the standard of living they enjoyed before they retired. This actually requires more income, not less. The reason is that the cost of living continues to go up each year. You might save money because you won't have to commute to work. You might have paid off the mortgage on your house. Even then, you will have other expenses to contend with.

For example, you may want to travel now that you have extra time. You might want to visit your children and grandchildren more. Additionally, almost all the current costs you have continue to go up in retirement (food, heat, cars, etc.). These costs add up to the point where you may be spending more in retirement, not less.

Many people are advised to save money in a pre-tax 401(k) retirement account. When they do so, they benefit from a tax deduction. People often believe that when they retire and begin to withdraw funds later in retirement, they will pay a lower tax rate. They think that because they are no longer earning a salary, they will be in a lower tax bracket. Unfortunately, usually the exact opposite is true. People often end up paying more in taxes in retirement because they must take RMDs. Often, that means they are taking out more than they need to, and this additional income can bump them up into a higher tax bracket.

That's where taking advantage of Roth conversions and putting the money into tax-free accounts can be highly advantageous.

As an aside: Usually, if I'm working with a client who is in their twenties, thirties, or forties, I typically advise them to save into a Roth IRA right from the start. That way, they benefit from thirty or more years of tax-free growth. In my mind, that is better than taxable growth.

Pension Options: Single Life, Joint and Survivorship, Lump Sum

As I mentioned in Chapter 3, far fewer people have pension options. If you do, consider yourself one of the few.

Single Life

Single-life options have the highest payouts. This can be the best option if you have no spouse, no children, and a lump-sum payment is unavailable or lower than feasible to take it. However, if you have a spouse, a joint and survivorship option can be advisable. With a joint and survivorship option, both you and your spouse can receive income from the pension. A joint and survivorship option might range from a 50 percent benefit to a 100 percent benefit.

Joint and Survivorship

The percentages refer to the proportion of the benefit the surviving spouse will receive. We typically recommend the 100 percent joint and survivorship option when selecting the income payout. Here's why. If one spouse passes away, the other spouse loses income from the lower of the two Social Security payments.

Let's say one spouse receives $40,000 a year from Social Security. Let's also say that the other spouse receives $30,000 a year from Social Security. If one spouse passes away, either remaining spouse will retain the $40,000 Social Security benefit and lose the $30,000. That's a substantial loss in income and the reason we recommend a 100 percent joint and survivorship pension for married couples taking the income option. Of course, the best course of action will differ for each of our clients and their pension plans.

Lump Sum

If a pension offers a lump-sum option, you can move the funds into any type of IRA investment that you'd like to. You can self-manage those funds. Perhaps there's an annuity on the market that may be able to increase your income stream compared to your pension or at least have a death benefit if you passed away early.

We take a close look at this. Many companies offering a pension work with just one insurance company. There are thousands of insurance companies, and one of them may be able to give you a higher payout.

Additionally, let's say you opted for the single-life payout or the joint life payout. Let's also say that you or both you and your spouse pass away one year later. The income from that pension is lost. However, that would not be the case if you have an income annuity with an outside insurance company. The income annuity is structured so whatever money is still in that account would pass to your beneficiaries and not be lost.

As you draw from an annuity, the value of that annuity decreases. When the annuity value reaches a certain level, you can Roth-convert that annuity and get tax-free income. Instead of withdrawing, let's say, $30,000 of income per year from a traditional IRA and paying taxes, you can take $30,000 and reduce the tax on that amount if withdrawing from a Roth IRA.

Supplemental Income: Preferred Stocks, Dividends, Annuities

There are various vehicles that we use to provide supplemental income. Preferred stocks are one option. A preferred stock is stock that pays a preferred dividend rate. There may be stocks that pay a 4 percent dividend, and that dividend can contribute to your income. Annuities, as I discussed in the previous section, can complement or replace some lost income from work.

Relying on preferred stocks and dividends can be risky. The return can change based on the companies you invest in. A national company that is also local to us, in the Lehigh Valley area, cut their dividend in half in 2020. The people who were relying on that company for income to be produced from their dividend had their income abruptly cut in half. Dividends, unlike annuities, are not guaranteed for life.

2. Designing a Retirement Plan

This is the stage of the process where your vision and our financial planning come together in a personalized retirement plan. Designing a retirement plan is often a unique experience for our clients. Frequently for the first time, they see what their savings can achieve and what goals they can have accomplished.

A client might have been saving for retirement from the time they started their first job. Now they might be sixty years old and seeing how their savings have accumulated. They might be seeing how much income they can live on in retirement. They might be seeing what strategies they can use to minimize their taxes. They might be learning where they can generate income from their investments.

As I said, seeing these things with your own eyes for the first time is not only illuminating but often exciting. It can be empowering to know that you can retire with confidence and enjoy the same quality of life or even better than you enjoyed during your working years. Many of our clients retire earlier than they would have otherwise after they see their options. Even if they do decide to continue to work, having the knowledge that they could retire sooner can be liberating.

Components of a Retirement Plan

In summary, designing a retirement plan is a process that begins with establishing your goals and what you would like to accomplish in your retirement. From there, we can determine how much income you need each year in retirement. Next, we look at how your investments are currently allocated. We also consider whether you're getting an appropriate return for the level of risk you can tolerate.

For many of the people who come in, the investments they have are simply not optimally aligned with their risk tolerance or return goals. Often, there are changes we can make to improve the overall portfolio. This is a process of rebalancing.

When we rebalance, we consider how the portfolio would perform if there was a market downswing. For example, if the market crashed by 50 percent as it did in 2008, would your portfolio go down by 50 percent or 25 percent? Is a drop of 25 percent within your risk tolerance threshold? If the most you could tolerate going down is 20 percent, and a stock market crash could mean a loss of 40 percent from the way the current portfolio is structured, we need to restructure the portfolio so it is back within the range of your risk tolerance.

A market crash is not something that happens once in a blue moon and never again. Stock market crashes are cyclical and have been occurring for a hundred years. According to an article from Morningstar, on average, every six to seven years the market goes down by 20 percent or more.[24] These events are something that we can prepare for and build into the structure of a portfolio.

The good news is that every time the market has crashed, it has fully recovered. The important thing is to make sure your portfolio can withstand the loss over time and that you have a place in your portfolio to draw income from when the markets are down.

Tax Strategies

Tax reduction strategies are another major component of the retirement plan. Your plan will use strategies that aim to minimize your tax burden over the course of your retirement. We look at your current tax burden. We look at whether your tax structure is more advantageous for Uncle

---

24 Emilia Fredlick, "What We've Learned From 150 Years of Stock Market Crashes," *Morningstar,* September 12, 2025, https://www.morningstar.com/economy/what-weve-learned-150-years-stock-market-crashes.

Sam or you. We look at your retirement accounts and your 401(k).

We consider whether your RMDs could force you into a higher tax bracket in your retirement years. If so, we use our tax planning software to try to get ahead of that by using Roth conversions and other tax planning strategies.

Other tax strategies that we have mentioned involve using a capital gains tax rate instead of ordinary income and distributing from the accounts tax efficiently. If you're charitably inclined, we can make sure that your gifting is taxed as little as possible. For example, we can use qualified charitable distributions that allow you to take money from your IRA without paying taxes and send it to your church or charitable organization. Neither you nor the charity has to pay the tax, and it can satisfy some or all of your RMD.

Estate Planning

Estate planning is a key component of retirement planning. Many people have no estate plan set up. Others have a plan, but it is twenty or thirty years old. A well-structured estate plan can make a huge difference to your beneficiaries when you pass away. The onset of retirement is a great time to revisit or update an estate plan.

If you wait until it's too late in your retirement to set up an estate plan, you might find yourself at an age where it is difficult to think clearly. Decisions might be harder. Setting up a will requires making well-thought-out decisions regarding what happens to your assets. It should be your decision, not the government's. If you do not have a will or beneficiaries, your assets will be distributed to whomever the law states is your next of kin instead of to those you want to give those funds to.

It is also important to consider who should make financial and healthcare decisions for you if you cannot make them yourself. Designate a power of attorney for finances and healthcare. Having these boxes ticked off for these critical items can bring you and your family peace of mind.

For some people, setting up a trust makes sense. There are many different types of trusts, but revocable trusts can be advantageous for those who own a home and plan to continue owning one.

Revocable Trusts

A revocable trust can be used to avoid probate costs, and it allows you to maintain control over the assets in the trust. For example, if you own a home and you pass away with the home in trust, your heirs can avoid the costly probate process (usually around 5 percent of the value of the property).

Now there are a lot of different types of trusts, but usually in early retirement it can make sense to have a revocable trust set up. And the way the ownership works is you still have control over the assets in the trust, but with that, you can protect your home or other real estate from probate costs. Probate is a legal process completed when a decedent leaves assets to distribute. The assets could be real estate, bank accounts, or financial investments. Probate may be required whether there is a will or not. However, it can be avoided if assets are placed in a trust or if accounts have named beneficiaries on them.

Probate can be both time consuming and costly. For instance, let's say that you own a $400,000 home and you pass away. Without a trust, your heirs would likely pay around 5 percent, or $20,000, in probate costs. If you set up a trust while you are living, you can still change any beneficiaries, sell the property, or purchase a new property. Your beneficiaries would have the added benefit of avoiding that $20,000 probate cost when you pass away.

Sometimes, I hear from people who were told not to purchase a trust because they either do not have enough money for the trust to be worth it for them or it just did not make sense for them. When I ask them who gave them that information, they tell me it was an attorney. Then, I ask them who they think the probate costs go to. They usually think it goes to the government. I explain to them that oftentimes, the probate costs go to the attorney. Sometimes even to the same attorney making the recommendation against getting the trust set up. This can be an undisclosed conflict of interest by the attorney that can end up gaining them a large sum of money while costing the client's children. This is another reason why it is critical to work with a fiduciary who is looking out for your best interest instead of their own. If you don't own a home and do not plan on purchasing one, you likely don't need a revocable trust.

To be sure, consult an estate attorney for the best advice for your specific situation.

For a significantly lower cost than the benefit (in this case, $20,000), you can set up a trust, move the home into the trust, set up a will, and designate powers of attorney to manage any medical directives. These are all components of estate planning that we help with for simpler estates.

Irrevocable Trusts

Irrevocable trusts are less common. They are primarily useful later in life or for larger estates. An irrevocable trust might be useful if you are in your eighties or nineties with early-onset dementia or a similar condition. Such a diagnosis might mean you are going to need home health care or nursing home care. An irrevocable trust can help to protect your assets from being seized by the nursing home.

After the assets are put into the trust, they are no longer in your name. You cannot easily make any changes to this trust or its assets because you are no longer the owner of those assets. The benefit of this type of trust, however, is that after a five-year look-back period, the nursing home cannot attach those assets to you. In essence, you have protected those assets from being seized by the nursing home so that they can be passed on to your beneficiaries.

Insurance Planning

Life insurance is popular, but not everyone has the right policy or needs the insurance they have. We conduct a detailed analysis for clients, and we find some commonalities.

For example, people often take out life insurance when they are young and healthy. The cost of the insurance in that policy is likely to be lower on that policy. However, the crediting rates for more current policies tend to be higher. In some cases, it makes sense to switch a policy to one that can have better crediting rates and, in some cases, even long-term-care protection.

We shop the market to find out what is the optimal insurance company for a client. We also look into long-term-care insurance. In some cases, we can wrap the long-term-care insurance into a life insurance policy so that a client gets the best of both worlds. Sometimes a stand-alone long-term-care policy is not the best option. Insurance providers can increase the premium and the amount you have to pay annually at their discretion.

I have had clients whose long-term-care insurance provider has increased their premiums by 30 percent in a given year. The same thing then occurred the following year. An increase of 60 percent within two years is substantial, not expected, and often not sustainable for a client to continue paying. Suddenly, long-term care is much less affordable.

Unfortunately, we see this type of situation just as clients are getting closer to the time they need the benefit from these long-term-care policies. The prices become out of control and difficult to afford. That's why it may be easier and more financially predictable by having long-term-care insurance wrapped in a life insurance policy.

With this type of policy, you have the advantage of a fixed premium that will not increase during your retirement. Another advantage is that if you don't use the long-term care, you don't lose all of the benefits. There is still a death benefit. If you pass away peacefully, having never needed the long-term care, your beneficiaries will receive the funds from the death benefit.

We also look at home and auto insurance. We do not sell these policies, and we do not review them to necessarily ensure you have the cheapest protection, but to ensure that you have the proper protections in place. If something happens, we don't want you to pay a huge amount out of pocket just to save a little on the premiums for your home and auto policies. In essence, we want to try to eliminate surprise misfortunes and reduce risk in retirement.

Retirement planning to us includes looking at all these factors, from auto insurance to estate planning. It's making sure you are set up properly, not just how you invest your funds.

Fees

Lastly, there is the question of fees. We want you to understand what your fees would look like if you decide to work with us.

Our clients often save money on fees by working together with us. One of the couples who came in were paying 2 percent per year in fees when we examined all of their investments and the associated companies. By working with us, they would pay significantly less. The numbers showed that this couple would pay $29,000 less in fees each year by working with us. Can you imagine having an extra $29,000 in your pocket each year just from savings in fees?

In this case, they had two variable annuities. For variable annuities, they assumed they were paying around 1 percent in fees. However, when we contacted the company, we found that they were paying many hidden fees for each annuity, which added up to around 3.5 percent in fees per year.

They also had a management fee of around 1.2 percent on their market investments. There were internal costs for the investments of over 0.5 percent as well. When we put the whole portfolio together, they were paying around 2 percent per year in fees.

They now had $29,000 more to spend and enjoy that they did not have to pay to a financial company or advisor.

Simply by conducting a fee analysis, we can often find hidden fees and determine if and by how much clients are paying more in fees than they need to. In some cases, we come out more expensive than what a couple or person is currently paying. We are transparent with our costs so you have a clear apples to apples comparison of our cost compared to what you are currently paying and can often show significant value behind what you are paying for.

Administrative Checks

There are also administrative items to check. For example, many people do not list beneficiaries on their investment accounts or bank accounts. These simple things can ensure a smooth transition of assets to your heirs, but only if they are taken care of and kept up to date as your life evolves. We work together with our clients so ensure a smooth transition of their funds financially. Our goal is to bring peace of mind to them and their families.

3: Our Gold Division

As your fiduciary retirement planner, we pride ourselves on providing what we call our "Gold Division."

Our Gold Division includes using sophisticated financial planning software to custom-design your retirement plan. We present recommended investments, including market risk investments and no-market-risk strategies. We create tax planning strategies to minimize taxes over your lifetime.

To complete your retirement planning, we offer estate and legacy planning. Using Monte Carlo simulations, we can show you the outcome of various scenarios that potentially include a sooner retirement or more income in retirement. We will work directly with you and an attorney to help you create or update wills, powers of attorney, trusts, and advance medical directives. We also strive to help you feel secure with long-term-care planning, home and auto insurance policies, and answers to your Medicare concerns.

Lastly, we will outline the fees you can expect to pay when working with us as well as the fees you are currently paying.

CLOSING WORDS

My goal with this book is to draw your attention to the importance of working with a fiduciary retirement planner.

A fiduciary retirement planner can create a custom-made retirement plan with you that considers your unique circumstances. They will take the time to understand your current lifestyle and your goals for retirement. A fiduciary planner will take you through a proven process to help you readjust your investments if necessary. They will make sure you have the right tools to minimize taxes and the right insurance in place.

Most importantly, a fiduciary retirement planner will suggest investments and a path forward that are in your best interest. All of this can help to bring you peace of mind. It can give you the confidence to know that you can retire and maintain your quality of life. In some cases, we may even be able to tell you that you can enjoy a better quality of life and you may be able to retire sooner.

We would love to welcome you as part of our family.

A family's legacy consists of many little moments, anchored by beloved traditions. The Guida family shares a meal each Sunday to connect and enjoy one another's company. You have your own traditions and aspirations, and it would be our privilege to work with you to strengthen your retirement plan and do our best to help ensure the coming years are as fruitful and enjoyable as they deserve to be.

If you are interested in working with a fiduciary retirement planner for your retirement planning needs, visit us at ABetterWayFinancial.com.

*I think a lot of people that go into opening
restaurants are all about the food, which I
am as well, but you learn very quickly that
it's all about the people.*
—Joanne Chang

APPENDIX

Financial Questionnaire

This comprehensive and confidential personal financial planning questionnaire is designed to help organize a sensible financial plan for your future. This may be filled out online, or if you prefer, you may print, complete, scan, and upload this document along with your statements when complete.

Recommended checklist of documents to upload to our secure shared drive:

- Your last 2 years of tax returns

- Recent annuity, life, and long-term-care statements

- Recent IRA, Roth, 401k, and brokerage account statements

- Recent savings and checking account values

- Employee benefit summary documents

- Social Security benefit statement (may be found at ssa.gov)

- Current financial plan

- Current income plan

- Current tax plan

Information Gathering:

	Client	Co-Client/ Spouse
Name		
Date of Birth		
Address		
City/State/Zip		
Email		
Cell Phone Number		
Working or Retired?		
Retirement Age Goal		

Family/Dependent Information:

(Please list all children, grandchildren, and dependents).

Names	Date Of Birth	Notes

Sources of Income:

Sources of Income	Client	Co-Client/Spouse
Wages (Salary and Bonuses)		
Other Income (Source?)		
Social Security Income (What Age?)		
Pension(s)		

Investments:

Please upload or send the most recent statements of your investments.

(You may black out any personally identifiable information).

Owner	Company Name	Account Type (IRA, Joint, Roth, 401(k), Etc.)	Amount/ Value Of Account	Investment Type (Bank, Brokerage, Annuity)	Drawing an Income (Yes Or No)?	Making Contributions?

Real Estate:

	Current Home Value	Amount Owed	Mortgage Payment	Interest Rate	Approx. Years Remaining on Mortgage	Income Producing? (Yes or No)
Primary Residence:	$	$	$			
Other Real Estate:						

Retirement Expense Form:

Life Insurance:

____

____

____

____

____

Long-Term-Care Insurance:

____

____

____

____

Retirement Goals:

How much AFTER TAXES are you going to need in retirement? (You may use the expenses that you currently have to come up with this number.) Be sure to include all debt payments, living expenses, and insurance payments that would continue into retirement.

If you're not sure how to calculate this figure, you may use the following formula:

Income–Taxes–Savings +/- any more or less you would like to have in retirement.

Living Expenses (Per Month)	Amount
Total Living Expenses	

Stay or Move Elsewhere in Retirement:

____

____

____

____

____

Future Significant Expenses:

____

____

____

____

Retirement Activities, Travel, etc.:

____

____

____

____

Legacy Goals:

____

____

____

____

Other Goals/Questions/Items to Share:

____

____

____

ABOUT THE AUTHOR

Frankie Guida has been affiliated with A Better Way Financial since 2016, helping retirees and pre-retirees prepare financially for a more stress-free retirement. His approach gives those he works with more confidence and guidance as they walk through their retirement.

Frankie is a Certified Financial Planner® professional and he has his Series 65 license. He is also a licensed Pennsylvania insurance agent for life, accident, and health insurances.

Aside from helping retirees and pre-retirees plan for a more successful retirement, Frankie enjoys spending time with his family and friends, playing sports, and giving back to his community. He enjoys giving back by being involved with his church, giving to various charitable organizations, educating the public, and mentoring other financial professionals.